SLIPPING INTO THE SHADOWS

SLIPPING INTO THE SHADOWS

Junkies, Prostitutes, Con Artists

Eugene Barron

iUniverse, Inc.
New York Lincoln Shanghai

SLIPPING INTO THE SHADOWS
Junkies, Prostitutes, Con Artists

iUniverse, Inc.

For information address:
iUniverse, Inc.
2021 Pine Lake Road, Suite 100
Lincoln, NE 68512
www.iuniverse.com

ISBN: 0-595-32764-8

Printed in the United States of America

Contents

Introduction: The Setting

This book documents the lives of not particularly nice people. A con man, pusher, murder, prostitute, victimizers and victims; they all give expression to the underbelly drama of New York. When I worked and lived in East Harlem I was curious about those who lived on the fringes of the straight world. My daily routine led to many encounters with the neighborhood people. Intrigued by a life style so distinct from my own, I tried to understand and paint the world through their eyes. Eventually I reached out beyond this impoverished community to criminal types who lived in better circumstances. But ultimately, social status or wealth didn't matter; they were all marked by destruction.

Whether conducting interviews in an abandoned building or in the chaotic street, I would try to quiet myself by thinking of a Buddhist meditation on the empty space between earth and sky. With screaming and yelling all around, junkies lurking in the darkness, I would breathe in a slow, deliberate manner as a counterpoint to watching life space filled with pain and rage. I encountered individuals with tortured psychics who in their own fashion adapted to a universe without rules or boundaries.

To many of us, these outsiders are "faceless", deviant creatures from another planet. We fear their presence and try to deny their existence. In New York, they are around the corner, either literally or figuratively, and like it or not, are very much part of the landscape. I have tried to capture their humanity by digging beneath the tough protective armor and have been struck by their coping capacities. I have allowed the protagonists to speak for themselves although the twists in their lives might defy the imagination of a gifted novelist. Despite the fact that most were severely abused in childhood and early adulthood, they maintained a "will" to survive. Still the very fact they were victims throughout their early lives, left deep, unhealed wounds. The concomitant anger drove them to compulsively destroy; striking out against themselves and those around them. Therefore it was not surprising to find lives rooted in fantasies of hate. Having been brutalized as children, the developmental default was self hatred, usually marked by addiction and violence. It didn't matter whether they were African-American, White, Latino, male or female, they were branded. Like Humpty Dumpty, they would put the broken pieces of their lives together but only to see it all fall apart. The cracks never disappeared but for some, finding meaning, either through education, child bearing or love, the pieces were gathered and change occurred.

As a recorder of the stories it was not easy to remain neutral after learning of their amorality and antisocial behavior. I asked myself should I make value judgments and simply label these people, "sociopaths" regardless of the cause of their character defects? I wondered if their faulty moral development reflected a failure of socialization?

For the most part, they were not provided with the supports of family, schools, peer groups or formal organizations as clubs or even organized gangs. Isolates, they neither fitted in, nor were they invited to join. Consequently they lacked the skills to make it in the "square" world. With a few exceptions, the conventional opportunity system, decent education and jobs, were mostly closed to them. The main recourse was provided by the deviant system of the criminal/addict subculture or an institutional subculture, found in the mental hospital or prison. On the everyday level, for the women it meant using their bodies as a commodity. For the men, it meant selling drugs or playing out con games as a way to earn their keep. As one of them noted, they simply were not meant to follow "the straight and narrow." I asked myself, does that excuse their antisocial actions? Maybe it had nothing to do with the "Officer Crumpky" syndrome a la West Side Story; bad parenting and societal injustice. Despite the fact that their home lives were marked by dysfunction, there were siblings who made it through. However there was a distinct quality to their upbringing compared to the siblings; for whatever reason they were chosen as the scapegoat in the family system. They lived out a self fulfilling prophecy; "once a victim, always a victim". Of course, the explanation might simply be reduced to biochemistry and low susceptibility to family and societal stress? There are many permutations to the nature and nurture issue of character development. Perhaps as one learns about their lives, the reader will arrive at his/her own conclusion.

In making contact and developing the interviews, as a psychotherapist, I was able to use my listening skills. In a way, I saw myself in the role of a social anthropologist entering an undeveloped country. I tried to gain a sense of their norms and values which were quite different then typical middle class or even working class mores. I encountered a deviant subculture where survival skills involve a high degree of manipulation and "acting out". The informants were in many ways atypical in that they were fairly sophisticated and articulate about themselves. A common denominator was that while all had sunk to the "bottom", none were willing to give up the will to live.

The recorded interviews were open ended which allowed for a free flow of thoughts and associations. Some of the meetings occurred over time, others were limited to a few encounters. Because I once lived in the area, had worked in the field of social work with this type of population, contacts were easily made and I felt safe in the interview setting. To find participants, I contacted social workers, spoke to street people and just spread the word. I was fortunate to meet individuals who despite their precarious life situations were willing to tell their tale.

In regard to the editorial work of the transcriptions, for the most part I had deliberately left out my questions and arranged the responses so that they formed a coherent story. While I rearranged comments and statements for reasons of continuity, I attempted to capture the essence of their narrative.

I have altered some of the background materials, such as names, for purposes of confidentiality. It was difficult to fully capture the expression of affect; the sobbing or anger that often occurred when points of suffering and pain were discussed. The experience for some was therapeutic and as Pablo explained, "it is the first time in my life that someone took the time to hear my story....it feels real good to get it all off my chest." Because they were willing participants, in a certain way it was cathartic. I didn't feel that I was a "peeping time" exploiting their need to vent. Though to be frank, on a certain level this middle class writer vicariously enjoyed listening to some of their outrageous exploits. On a deeper level, I genuinely liked them but I found it difficult to reconcile this feeling with the history of their violent actions. I resolved this dilemma by reminding myself that each one of them, in their own way, were struggling to create a new life.

1

Confessions of a Con Man

It was a chance encounter with Les in a coffee shop on the Upper West Side that gave me a glimpse of the shadow world of the con man. Rapping about poetry, we developed a nice rapport. Admittedly, there was part of me fascinated by the "sociopath" life style; not the violent types but those who lived by their wits. I confessed to him, perhaps the kernels of psychopathology were also within me; the difference was that I did not act them out. We were in agreement that amorality contaminated much of America and was not confined to the streets. Hitting it off, we made a date to meet again at my office.

Initially I was tense since this was not to be the standard therapy session. Arriving exactly on time, confident and verbal, Les made it clear he wasn't here for psychotherapy but had a need to unload. The story that unfolded was more like a confession and I played the part of a listening priest. Curious and perplexed, I wondered how this short, slightly overweight, well groomed gentleman, could be the monster he claimed.

I was startled by the texture and style of his presentation, because Les appeared to be a subdued, middle class guy but if I closed my eyes, I heard the voice of a rapid speaking, ghetto hipster. It was a leap to conceive that this soft spoken man was a product of crime and brutality. His tale was kind of a cosmic joke of an unusual role reversal; a youth from a Hassidic family who entered the rabbit hole, squeezing into the Black underworld.

The "mouth" as he was known on the streets, was a type of "invisible man"; a white man internalizing the marginal part of ghetto life and using it to foster a criminal life of revenge and abuse. He destroyed those who trusted him. He betrayed those who believe in him. Despite existing in a Bosch contorted world, there were also seeds of decency. Later in his life, the seeds allowed him to be influenced by a Jewish predilection for education and respond to the role model of an ex-junkie friend's call for salvation.

Jews Without Money

My parent went to Ecuador to escape the holocaust where I was born. They eventually made their way to Brooklyn and settled in the Bedford Stuyvesant. It was important for them to be there because my father was a follower of the Lubovitch sect which was located nearby. While today the area is predominately Black, then it also included a melting pot of Jews, Italians and the usual white trash. It hasn't change; it was the pits then and it is still the pits. Garbage was thrown onto the streets and sidewalks were permeated with cat piss and dog shit. Here I was in America, "the land of the free", but in my home it was an Eastern European ghetto. Yiddish was our family tongue and I didn't learn to speak English until I entered school. My father lamented that he couldn't afford to send me to "cheder" (Hebrew school) and tried to teach his version of Judaism.

While I am not sure how I felt toward my mom, I loved the old man. Yea, despite all the beatings, he did things for me that the average father would never do. I would ask and he would rarely refuse. For example, I loved baseball and he couldn't tell a baseball from a hockey puck. Yet when I would say "pop, take me to the baseball game" and if needed, he would borrow the money for us to go. Upon arriving, he might stand for the Star Spangled Banner, then sit down and sleep until the game's end. Then I would wake him to take me home. I enjoyed planes and I would suggest, "pop, let's go to the airport and watch the planes take off." We had no car and despite the difficulty of a long schlep with buses and subways, we would go. How many fathers would do that for their kids?

In my heart, I knew he loved me, though he often beat the shit out of me. It was just that he had difficulty, big time, expressing loving feelings. When he let down his guard, he had a way of looking that indicated he cared; sometimes it seemed he was even proud of me. This became evident to me when the school classified me as "retarded". The guidance teacher called my mother aside on open school week and informed her that I was "mentally limited". I am not sure of the reason for the problem. Maybe I seemed slow because we spoke Yiddish at home and English was my second language. In addition, I rarely paid attention to those pathetic teachers who tried to teach me by rote memory. My mother, the poor woman, didn't know what that label meant and asked my older sister. I remember overhearing her response, "he is slow and is brain is not normal". They claimed my IQ was 60; meaning "I was stupid". The officials recommended that I be placed in a special school for retarded kids. When the old man returned from work, I heard her whisper "the teachers say he is slow in the head". When she whispered, "he is mischugina", pointing to my head, I was really hurt but didn't show it. My father argued, raising his voice, "I know my son; what are you talking about, he is a bright kid". In turn, my mother who was the boss inside the home, shrugged her shoulder, "what do we know; the school people say he is stupid and needs to go to a special school. She added, "anyhow, I always figured there was something wrong with him; now I know." My father collapsed on the thread, worn couch, choked up, yelled back, "he is a thief, a liar, maybe a crook one day, but he is not stupid."

They were at an impasse and my aunt was consulted. They were unable to resolve the question of my intelligence but they agreed it would be a "shunda" (humiliation) to brand me retarded by allowing the transfer. My father never convinced them but rather it was the family fear of shame that forced their decision. You see, in a strange way, pride and shame was the major motivating force that influenced their reactions. The old man beat me when my behavior brought shame to either him or the family. Unfortunately for them, whenever I wished to hurt them, "shame was my revenge". For example, I would get in trouble and he would be forced to leave work to meet the guidance counselor. At home, feeling humiliated, he would vent his fury and there would be vicious cycle. fights and rebellion In looking back I wondered why I received most of the beatings compared to my brother and sisters. Sure my older brother was hit but never severely beaten. Since we were twelve years apart I didn't know him very well. He was a regular guy; made his way through college but was drafted and somehow ended up in the Marines. He died in the Korean War; what a waste. My older sister was a genius and had it easy. She learned several languages, received a doctorate and obtained a high position at the U.N. My kid sister was more like me; we both were Americanized. Though frequently in trouble, my father never laid a hand on her. She also ended up a dope fiend but that is another sad story.

The divisions in the family were because of our different roots. My parents and older siblings were from Europe and therefore our perspectives and values were far apart. I would listen to my brother criticize our black neighbors, calling them "low life schwartzes living in shit". Even though I was younger, I would speak up, reminding him, "what do you mean; do you think we live in a royal palace here?" He would insist "we're better". I remember responding in a mocking tone, "how mother fucker? We still wipe our asses with newspapers. We can't afford toilet paper. How are we so different then them?" He answered, "you don't understand…I can't talk to you," lowering his voice in despair, "no one can reason with you". In a way he was right.

I know people stereotype Jews that we are all wealthy. We certainly didn't fit the picture. We were one step above the poverty line but maintained the illusion we were better then those other poor suckers. When the old man actually had a job and was not on strike or laid off, he pulled in only three hundred a week. I remember when I was 14 and he was without work, I supported the family. I easily made over seventy dollars a day playing con games; "Murphys", "Badgers" and that kind of shit. To add to the till, I also was a "runner" for bookies and "bagged" numbers. The family's reaction was so hypocritical, it drove me crazy. When he was without work and the family needed the money that I supplied, nobody asked about the source. Only when he found work did he question me. To my way of thinking, life had castrated him. Because my measure was the "big buck", I viewed him as a less of a man then the street hustlers.

I had mixed feelings about the old man. There was a bond, but the anger kept us apart. To be honest, I was a fucking, angry kid. Even as a youngster, I resented hearing his "bullshit"; his repetitious lecture themes, "if you work hard, stay on the straight and narrow, then the good life will be yours". My unvoiced thoughts would be, "so you worked along the straight and narrow, where the hell has it gotten you?"

Our family was entangled in a web of poverty. It stunk and I believed he was responsible. I was exasperated; ignoring our impoverishment, the old man seemed to be from another planet. We didn't even have a television. It didn't matter to him; he never even went to the movies. Because his English was so poor, he rarely listened to the radio except for the Yiddish station. Most of his life was deprivation; marginal in Europe, South America and then Bedford Stuyvesant. Of course he realized that we had less then others, but fatalistically, he figured that it was God's will. He had his own high standards and code of honor; no way did it mesh with mine.

A Fucking, Angry Kid

The conflict between our values led to daily beatings. It didn't help that his arms were like tree trunks. At one time he worked as a printer and whipped heavy galleys that weighed over 200 pounds. When he slapped, it was a blow that could throw me across the room; that was for something minor. If furious, he would clench his fists and loose himself in a flying rage.

I recall an incident which I would consider a serious example of his fury. In preparation for my Bar Mitzvah we went down to the Lower East to purchase a suit. Later we visited my aunt and I was forced to wear this dark, somber looking outfit. The suit to him was precious. I had a single suit, one tie and dress shirt; that was it. I decided to take a break and play outside. Before I left, he scowled and warned me to care for the clothes. In the street, I got roped into a touch, football game and returned with a torn jacket. There were consequences; a five punch performance which laid me in the hospital for a week with a broken nose and ribs. He twisted my hand so hard that the wrist was broken but I refused to learn. I was stubborn.

Where was my mother in all this? In most homes, a mother would protect their kids from brutality; not in mine. She never laid a hand on me but worked "hand and glove" with him. For example if she learned I stole, she would warn me of my father's anger. She would even cry while I was stomped. The tears were confusing; on the surface she seemed to care but in fact, provoked the beatings by slyly "cutting his balls off". For example, she might complain "he stole from Mrs. Katz up the block" and when his fury was red hot, yell "you're not a man if you don't show him who is boss". No wonder I preferred the streets.

I finally got fed up after a vicious beating which ended in a concussion. I refused to go to the hospital because it was useless. Sure I could complain of child abuse but this would only shame him and result in another revolving, door beating. At the age of 15 it dawned on me that I could not survive living that way.

It was on Yom Kippur, the Day of Atonement. The old man instructed me to arrive at the synagogue by 6:00 AM. Instead I showed up at noon, fearfully watching his scowling face. In a tantrum, he pushed aside the chairs, rushed at me and punched so hard that I flew across the middle isle. Ironically, I landed on a plaque acknowledging the "loving memory" of somebody and fell flat on my face. Later after returning home, he grabbed my lapel, pulled his arm back to strike and I knew this meant a visit to the hospital. Then and there, I decided this was the end of the abuse; no more concussions. Looking directly into his eyes, I yelled, "this time you are not going to do a number on me; not this time. You can have the first punch but you better make sure you kill me because if I am still standing, I'll kill you." Man was he in shock when he heard this. He couldn't believe his ears. He yelled back, "despite everything you've done, you were never disrespectful to me". I yelled back, "I'm tired of being used for a fucking punching bag. I've had it up to here with your shit." He ordered me out of the house and with twenty dollars in my pocket, I left. I carried my few belongings in an old, rotten bag that they had once dragged from Russia. I completely cut myself off and never returned.

I realize in looking back that it was not just the beatings which got to me but the lack of contact. It was incredible that we were six people living in three rooms and we would walk by each other without ever connecting. There was an imaginary traffic light that would blimp "stop" or "go" as we passed. I was never caressed or hugged by my mother or sisters; that wasn't surprising because my parents never showed warmth or fondled each other. Forget about affection; we were starved. My father would blush if he noticed a couple kissing. The old man was a Hassid and some people are under the illusion that they are expressive; maybe at religious celebrations but certainly not at home. They seem to believe they are supposed to hold back and wait until they enter God's heaven. Meanwhile on this earth, everything remains private and hidden. Living in a world without joy, hiding anger and denying feelings, something broke inside me. I was alone in that house and after I left, alone on the street. Eventually all the pain and emptiness led to dope.

Living on the Streets

Running from home, I trudged to Prospect Park which was a few miles away. I slept there and later in the subway. I was real hungry but afraid to return to the block. I thought the old man had notified the police and if I was brought back, I would receive a super beating. I was determined not to return. Eventually, I found my way to Washington Square Park in the village. That is where I met Linda or rather she picked me up.

She was 29, fourteen years older, and was searching for someone to share her weird, sexual fantasies. Linda was plain looking, heavy set and had a strong sensual disposition. I was desperate and though the experience started out exciting, it badly ended. After a few months, she made weird sexual demands on me. It is too upsetting to remember it; she was really sick. It was a lot of kinky and freaky stuff.

It was about that time I experimented with drugs but not with her. She would find my "works" and exclaim, "naughty, naughty", which captured the flavor of how she might be aroused. In order to keep sane, I knew I had to leave. She went crazy when I told her it was time to split. She talked about marriage and that convinced me she was a lunatic; wanting to team up with a teenager. She drove me nuts with her perversions and I now realize the sexual fantasy stuff left a bad imprint. Even after I was gone, it felt as if my head was screwed on backwards. I paid some heavy dues with that lady; very heavy dues.

The Con

To survive on my own, I depended on my street smarts and the ability to con. Those skills, if you want to call them that, helped me survive as a "junky". Preparation for the life of hustling began when I was only eleven. You might think that was young but it was late compared to other kids who started as early as seven. One learned the skills from older friends. For example, Bob (today, a professor of physics), taught me how to do the "Murphy", a prostitution con game. Rope a "meatball" and tell him you can connect him to a sexy "trick" that will only cost seventy five dollars for the girl and the room. I would suggest for his protection against being ripped off by the girl, he temporarily leave his money in an envelope that was secure with me. I would lead him into a hallway, excuse myself for a minute and disappear through a roof door or a back exit. Usually the "mark" was too embarrassed to report the incident to the police. Another hustle was ripping off people as they left the bank. There I worked with a team. One of us would identify a "mark" and approach her with the story of finding a wallet which seemed to be stuffed with money. I would persuade the "mark" that she is part of the find and before it is divided, each party puts up money as security with the third "innocent" party holding the funds. The process is somewhat complicated, but the bottom line is the sucker ends up with an envelope stuffed with paper. I even recall once ripping off a frail, elderly lady for several hundred bucks. Then it didn't matter but now I am not proud of it.

The "short-change" game was my specialty. One asks for fifty dollars worth of change at a counter. Then engage the teller in a continual, money exchange; the dough flies back and forth and pretty soon I have most of the money while the teller is left with a few bucks.

A similar con was the "quick peck" exchange which means "pecking" the cash register. For example, I buy candy for fifty cents and give the cashier a ten dollar bill. Then the fun starts; money flies back and forth and at the end almost all the money is in my pocket.

I was far from a sweet guy and some might consider me ruthless but I maintained certain standards, mostly against violence and direct stealing. I took pride in my skills as a con artist and believed petty thievery was beneath me. At times I worked with pimps and would steer "Johns" to their girls but I never directly ripped them off. In all the years of hustling, I never racked a head. Sure I carried a knife for protection or to threaten, but I never used it. On the street like in any society, there is a hierarchy. I considered myself above the average criminal because I relied on my persuasive abilities. I believed anybody who needed to use violence was a "stupid scumbag". I now realize that because I felt like a "shit", I needed to make myself superior by looking down on those who seemed lower then me.

What type of person would rip off an old lady? Obviously for me, it was not to gain wealth but a more powerful force; drugs. By the age of eighteen, I had a small twenty-five dollar a day habit. That was nothing compared to a year later when I needed two to three hundred dollars, daily, to support the craving. Can you imagine what it is like to gather that type of money every day, seven days a week?

The craving and associated demands didn't occur overnight. At first I only snorted "shit" (heroin) and popped pills. Soon I realized that mainlining was a better trip and I was hooked. "Hooked" is a powerful compulsion and it meant that my daily, life's obsession was to raise money for the "golden arm". Literally, the entire day from early morning to the last thing I did at night, was to "cop". I was like a squirrel, sometimes saving a few bags for the next morning because I didn't want to wake up empty. The need to "score" drove me to hustle with a frantic fervor. Ironically when I finally scored, I was often too wasted and strung out to enjoy my success.

For a while I supported the habit by dealing. I worked for a dude named "Slick Sam" who ran a heroin factory. He would give me a piece of the action if I pushed his product. During that time, I did everything but beat people over the head. It is hard to imagine living with such a craving. It wasn't even day to day; the need was almost hour to hour. When I was strung out bad, my twenty four hour job was getting a fix. At times it would seem I would go without sleep for two or three weeks. My mind only worked in terms of money and "junk"; getting the cash and making the connections. I remember sitting in a shooting gallery of low life junkies, nodding out and thinking that "I've had enough. I need to get my pokes together and go back to the folks". I thought, "I ain't never going back to this shit again". That lasted the forty five minutes it took to get off the high and then I was back to the usual scene. My life was totally entangled by the heroin web.

Hovering in the background, waiting, were the "pigs". I rarely got busted for the con games; it was always drug possession. They knew when I was dirty and whenever they wished could pick me up. I would do "soft time" which in essence meant popping in and out of jail, usually at the House of Detention. In prison, my craving continued. Even there I was able to score from some of the guards, once paying a "fucking pig", as much as two hundred dollars. Life was a ping-pong game, in and out of prison.

The "Mouth"

I know there is a black intonation to my voice when I shift into the hustling mold. Although I am white, my scene was with the black underclass. On the streets, most of my buddies were black. Whenever I was out there, I would talk like those "mothers". In the "slam", my friends were black. They used to call me "Harry Honky". They accepted me, not because of muscle but they recognized my gifts as a con man. To them, I was also known as the "mouth". The "mouth" was the guy who could persuade a hungry dog leaving a butcher store, to give up the meat. I was respected because when there was a "panic", which meant a dope shortage, I was the guy who could score. You see, when the panic occurs you've got a lot of sick dope fiends out there and they will sell their own mothers. I just continued to do my regular thing. I could encounter a guy walking down the street with ten dollars and soon he would be left with a deuce. I was capable of pulling a "short change" anywhere in the city, confident that in twenty minutes I would end up with ninety percent of the money.

Of course this life style wasn't simple. Most of the time I avoided the cops but it was tough to deal with the street, wise guys. Once a few "meatballs" caught me and I paid heavy dues. It was a Harlem bar and the owner knew what was happening, but played cool. Glancing at the bar tender, I noticed he made a sign to his buddy and I sensed the game was up. I wanted to split but it was too late. I tried talking my way out but it didn't work. I was worried he had a gun behind the bar. I attempted to slowly shift toward the exit but this time the "mouth" didn't come through. I was convinced this was my last day on this earth. The other dude was waiting behind me. I pulled out my blade, swung around but missed. I then managed to run around him toward the door but it was jammed. I was holding onto the knob when I felt their paws on me. They dragged me out into the alley through a back door. They beat and cut me up bad; stuffed me into an ash can and slammed the fucking lid. The next morning I woke up to the sound of an alley cat. Bloodied and practically crippled, I crawled out like some form of a roach. The police found me staggering on the street and dropped me off at Harlem hospital. It took two months to recover but still I didn't learn.

I Hardly Felt Guilty

I hardly felt guilty when I was part of the "life". I rationalized that the meatballs I hustled were meant to be used. Still, no matter how far gone I was there were some actions that I deeply regret and really experience shame.

Frequently, I had no place to live. I was like a wolf roaming the streets, concealing my razor, sharp teeth. Crossing 72nd street, in an area once known as "needle park", I noticed a middle aged, blind woman making her way. When she hesitated at the curve, I offered assistance. The gesture to help was authentic but when I learned she lived alone, the wheels turned. It wasn't long before I manipulated my way into her life and move into her pad. She lived in a lovely brownstone off Riverside Drive. It was quiet and serene and I had it made.

I persuaded her that I was a college student in need of a residence. She was under the illusion that she had found companionship with an educated, young man. In fact, I never completed high school but my advantage over most street people was an interest in reading and a sophisticated vocabulary. It was easy to pass for straight.

Gladys was plain looking, pleasant and quite nice. I was the first man in her life. I conned her to believe that after graduating, I intended to attend medical school and asked her for financial help. Everything was a lie; even the false name I gave her. I even offered to marry her and promised the gift of a "seeing eye" dog. To ease her into the con, I would borrow small sums, then a few hundred and then a thousand. I ripped her off for several thousand dollars; her complete savings. Because this was done in a gradual fashion, Gladys didn't realize she was being cheated. When her account was empty, I even sold her stereo. In my view, it was for a good cause; feeding the habit. I disappeared with "no good-byes" in search of my next prey. In retrospect I know it was cruel but then it didn't matter.

Port Authority is the Mecca for a lot of young kids from the hinterlands. They arrive with ice cream on their face. I was the wolf in "sheep's clothing", ready to devour them to support the habit. One evening while hanging out, I noticed a lovely, almost luminous young lady strolling through the terminal. She was carrying two worn bags and I offered assistance. We struck up a conversation and she explained she was from Kansas and had arrived to study acting. To me, she was beautiful, fresh and clean. It was as if the Wizard of Oz, dropped Dorothy onto my lap. At first my motivation was merely to have this beautiful person by my side. Because Laura was so naïve, it was easy to persuade her to stay with me. Even after several months living together, she was unaware I was an addict. Laura's vision of a "dope fiend" was that of a monster and she was literally stunned when she first caught me "shooting up" in the bathroom. She didn't know how to react. I tried to persuade her it was a temporary condition but I knew it was useless to continue to deny my addiction. Sadly for her, she remained with me.

Laura's gradually slipped into the "life". When I was "bummed out" I would persuade her to make the connection and pick up the dope. She was reluctant but because she felt sorry or was in love, it was easy to overcome her resistance. She would then visit these horrible haunts to get the shit. One dreary day when she was down, she whispered, "I want a taste". Maybe because I cared, I first tried to discourage her but we both had a destructive streak; she soon got strung out. One faithful day when we were "short", she volunteered to walk the street. Thereafter,

I encouraged her to peddle her ass for both of us. Almost every night she walked her beat. I admit, I was "bad news", often faking sickness, pressing her to spend extra hours out there to raise money. Returning home, she would give me the money; then cook, clean and finally exhausted, flop herself onto the mattress.

It was tragic; she was like a loyal dog in love with a cruel master. It was even worst when she slid downhill. Often sick and needing more and more dope, she became a liability. I just threw her out. Or rather, I changed the locks and told her not to return. By this time she was far gone and ended up with one of those low down, street pimps; not that I was much better. One day she was found dead in an alley way; her throat cut wide open. I ask myself how callous could I have been to sink so low? It was not even conscious but automatic; a way of life. Deep inside, I felt like a piece of "crap" and I needed to drag everyone who cared for me down to the cesspool. I rationalized my behavior with the notion that the world was a "big rip off". I avoided guilt because on the streets I felt that I lived in a special universe; "it's them against me". Among us, we understood that another junky is just a piece of meat to be ripped off. As for the junky chicks, they were considered pieces of meat, hanging on a hook.

Super Con Men

I had both nerve and was grandiose in my guise of the "con man". I deluded myself that I was the best and the greatest. In fact, I was small time and no match to the pimps who practiced the ultimate con; to manipulate and control the soul of another.

On the street, they were labeled, "players" but to my way of thinking, they were just con men playing with the "heads" of women. The small time operators handling one or two girls were called "popcorn" pimps. I recall a "popcorn" pimp who pulled an average of a thousand dollar a day from his two women. This dude was called "Mr. Clean" because he was so fastidious; he owned a Cadillac, a great pad and a wardrobe that was out of sight. The big time operators might have a dozen girls in their stables.

"Mr. Love" would be considered a successful pimp. He was great looking and very smooth. At his high point he had twenty working girls. His life style seemed to illustrate the American success story. He had a magnificent house, dozens of cars and great wardrobe; you name it, he had it. Although he loved cocaine, he was smart enough never to get "strung out". He was wise because he left the "life" while ahead, married and raised a family; still once a "con man" always a "con man". Although he had only an eighth grade education, he was able to transfer his street talents to the straight world, telling people what they wish to hear. The "fucking dude" barely literate, became a director of a counseling program, instructing people how to live their lives. To me he was a super con artist. Dig it, he even conned me; he was a con man's, con. He was the Ph.D. of the con men. For example, after release from prison, I bumped into the "cocksucker" in Harlem. I had only ten bucks in my pocket. He was wearing a long, leather coat, leather this and that, looking rich. He warmly greeted me with a huge hug. Before I realized it, he persuaded me to lend him the ten, rapping that he was temporarily short and promised within an hour, twenty-five in exchange. He was great with his promises. Of course the money never materialized, yet I still remain fond of him. Later, because of the facade of respectability and his street experience, he ended up on the Attica commission. Once I attempted to visit him at his office and he suggested I leave. He explained that it didn't look good in his present position for to be associated with ex-cons still on the streets. The irony was he ended up on that commission and I ended up at Attica. It was in prison, the most intense experience in my life, that turned me around.

Surviving Jail

The first thing to do upon entering a tough prison is to establish a "rep"; either you persuade the convicts not to mess with you or the alternative, be destroyed. I knew I needed to create a tough, violent image.

It was my second day in the "joint" and all I can think of was not to be made someone's "woman". I preplanned a script to save myself. Standing on the lunch line, I turned on an innocent dude behind me. I screamed, "you son of a bitch take the tray" and smashed it into his face. As he went down, I stomped on him. The other prisoners started shouting and screaming and finally the "screws" grabbed and dumped me in the "key lock" for sixty days; essentially restricting me to the cell This was better then the alternative of the "box" which is solitary confinement. There if the "goons" find you difficult, they just beat the shit out of you. The "goons" are a special group of guards who act as the "heavies to deal with the "bad ass dudes".

I went far enough to establish my "rep" which gave me certain privileges such as selecting a "woman". This means a pick of the "freshies". They are easy to spot; new prisoners who aren't street tough. The message to the newcomer is "either become my "woman" and mine alone, or you get gang banged". If he refuses, you set him up; organize a "gang bang". After such an experience the "freshy" is more than happy to join you.

Prison does strange things to people. I am not "gay" and there are no more homosexuals in prison then outside. I acted that way for two reasons; to satisfy my sexual needs and to protect myself from becoming someone else's "woman". For me the key to survival was to convince those around me that I was crazy and not to be messed with. I paid a price; a loss of a sense of myself. In my past life, I was never violent or interested in sex with men. In prison, I was a nobody; a number.

The only prisoners exempted from many of the pressures were the Mafia guys. They lived on the top and were above it all. They never had to worry about being "broken". But that didn't exclude them from the biggest danger to sanity in prison life; boredom. We would all spend time watching T.V.; it was our link to both fantasy and to the outside. For some reason it was often on the soaps. It was weird to hear these tough "low lifes'" in the mess hall after the soap, discussing "did you see what happened to Mary today; do think he got her knocked up...I wonder what her mother-in-law is going to do tomorrow?"

I stayed pretty much a "loner" while doing time. The library became an important part of my life and whenever I was free, I read. Gradually there was shift and I matured. Reflecting on the waste in my life, I decided that after my release, I would no longer "shoot up". To help prepare myself, I enrolled in a college program, studied psychology, hoping to discover answers about myself. I grew to recognize that my life needed to have meaning. It was not an easy decision; the drug attraction was and is always strong. I've known guys who were in prison twenty years, out on the street one day and they score. I didn't want to be one of those guys yet I couldn't trust myself. Once released, I tried an agency but they insisted I go into a closed system which to me was like being in "lock up". "No way", I complained, "I just did my time bro and I'm not doing more".

Shopping for Love

Broke after two weeks out of prison, I had nothing, not even a place to live. I was on the way back to "junk". Walking down Broadway, shivering on a frigid New York winter day, I decided to sign into Phoenix House. After twenty-four hours, it reminded me of my strict prison life and I signed out. Fortunately, I later bumped into an old "ex-junky" friend; "cool Nat", who was a director of a program at Reality House. He noticed that I had "shot up" and it looked like I was going to again dig myself in a hole. He invited me to check the place out.

I trekked with him up to this dumpy office in an old brownstone and there he explained that the program was a good place to work through my "crazies". I avoided his eyes and started making excuses but Nathan had been around, was a hip dude and saw through my act, exclaiming, "look man, your going to walk away from me and your gonna flip and flop and that street out there is gonna gobble you up". Trying to weasel out, I explained that "I was shopping". He laughed, "what you shopping for; you want someone to love you?" That made me nervous but he was relentless; "my man, you look like you need someone to love you; well I loves you". He raised his voice real loud; "I love you like my brother;". Then this huge, burly dude, got up, grabbed my face and kissed me smack on the lips. Wow, I was really confused and I braced myself to hit him but he raised his fists and warns, "don't start anything you can't finish. I am a lot older than you mother fucker and much tougher. I'll take your head and it will fly out the window and go splat on the pavement. Listen, you honky mother, you sit down here and dig what I got to say to you bro. I want you to hear me loud and clear." Nathan warned me "once a dope fiend, always one for the rest of your life. It will always be in the blood but you can fight it and stop shooting up the shit". He persuaded me to enter into a methadone program and connected me to an in-hospital "detox" program.

After two weeks, I returned to Reality House and joined its program. Somehow Nathan's "tough love" woke me up from my stupor; life changed. In prison, I had received a high school degree and had taken several college courses. At Reality House, I participated in the morning activity and in the afternoon, I attended college. I was able to receive special grants and even obtained a scholarship for tuition. I was fortunate to also receive help from the Fortune Society which assists ex-cons.

I busted my ass to become a college graduate. I was real "puffed up" when Nathan then demanded, "now you are going for your Masters". "Bullshit" I respond, "I have been averaging 22 credits a term and I've had enough. I want to play".

Nathan was a hard guy and he pushed me into going on to Columbia where I studied psychology. While in school, I continued to work as a therapist at Reality house. There I lived rent free. In addition earning a living was wonderful, especially handling "clean" money. I felt clean for the first in my life and like a ripple effect, there were other changes. I stopped dressing like a low life. Becoming more professional, even my speech style and language changed. My relationships also altered; where before I associated mostly with female junkies or ex-junkies, I started going out with straight women. Gradually I found myself more at home in the square culture then the street world. In fact, I became so dissociated from that world that I did a poor job as a counselor. I was asked to leave. That was fine because I knew that I didn't wish to belong to that world; it was no longer me.

Out on my own, I still didn't know who I was. Not fully comfortable with the middle class world, I became political. I joined Marxist, fringe groups, jumping from one to another. It wasn't easy but eventually I settled down as a counselor and started to write. The biggest change was for the first time in my life, "I dug myself". I had gotten into respecting and loving "me" and that was the most wonderful gift. Drugs could never substitute for that.

Reflections

Since childhood I've been "fucked up the ass" and I still need to come to terms with a lot of the residual anger. I am well aware that I could have continued to be like those junky suckers out there. I know that there is a destructive need to hold onto and act out my anger, which will push me off the cliff. There is no one who knows better then me that there exists within me a raging time bomb ready to explode. I remember how it feels to be so low that I could easily float down the sewer when it rains. I know what it is like to sit shivering with a "spike" in the arm, one step ahead of the man. When I bottomed out, I realized I could no longer live that way. Still I have not forgotten who and what I was. I believe that I am no longer that psychopathic, con man. Maybe it is a fantasy, but I just love being alive. I want to live. I want to be with people who care.

To be honest, I recognize the old needs and habit remain in the shadows. Part of me still tingles when I pass by my old haunts. In a perverse way, part of me misses the life of hustling and shooting up. Sometimes sitting alone in the night, I am depressed and feel the old urge "to get off. I start deluding myself what it was like to be on the stuff and how good it felt to be high. Like many junkies, I was there due to the "head trip". Because of the continual crises, in a strange way the trip was exciting; never boring. Being compulsively driven, my personality like many junkies, craved the excitement of living on the edge. Of course there were heavy dues to be paid but now I no longer have the desire to pay them.

It has been several years since I last "spiked". It was as if I am reborn and given a second chance. It is the present that is important and I try to make the most of it. There is not much I take for granted. I am well aware that I sold part of my life and others down the river but I came back. I feel in my heart if ever again I cannot control the urge, rather then stick another spike in my arm, I will jump off the Brooklyn Bridge. I am convinced that if I shoot up even once, everything that I have accomplished will go down the drain; it would all have been for nothing.

2

"I Wish I Had Done More of It in My Life"

Barbara somewhat frail, of delicate built and despite the fact that she is in her mid thirties, looks about twenty-five. She has a plain but attractive quality to her. She speaks rapidly, easily smiles, jokes and is articulate but not pedantic despite the fact that she has three advanced degrees. She rarely slips into street argot though she has been living on the fringes of society for a good part of her adult life. One might mistake her for a conventional, young lady, who enjoys intelligent conversation and good company. The image though is deceptive; if one tunes in, it is rather easy to notice the inappropriateness of her emotional tenor. The affect is flat. She will talk about today's dinner, illness or death in the same non emotional, nondescript tone. She discusses life as if she is watching a T.V. program; disengaged and disconnected. It is as if her life history merely consists of a series of adventures.

While she is certainly charming and pleasant, maybe the emotional discontentedness is the secret of her ageless, youthful appearance. Still her tale is worth telling for she lived out the flip side of the "lower depth" street life; glamorous but still empty.

The Fast Life

I have been involved in smuggling, selling drugs, fraud, prostitution and sex orgies but I don't consider myself unusual. It is just the life I choose and unlike those on the street, I always came out on top. I recognize the contradiction between my having advanced degrees, including a doctorate (art history), traveling throughout the world, fluent in several languages and the life of the hustler but what can I say; all are me.

There is no accounting for my life. My younger sister and parents are rather plain. They are just a nice middle class, Brooklyn family. My father never reached his potential, having once been a writer but put it aside after becoming an alcoholic while tending bar. He also acted in bit parts and found gigs in T.V. Now his regular job is that of a bell hop and it is sad to think of a man his age and background doing this for a living. Still both parents treated me well and I don't hold them accountable.

On the other hand, my mother's unmarried, sister Tilda was a strong influence. Although I had a much younger sister, I was treated very special by her; spoiled like an only child.. Aunt Tilda, in a way was my surrogate mother. I guess the "split" in my life style reflected the contrast between my conventional parents and erratic life with her. Because aunt Tilda had no children, she took me under her wing. We would travel together. In the winter, it would be Florida. I noticed there were a number of wealthy boyfriends who treated her like a queen. I always had a feeling they were underworld types since several of them died violent deaths. That didn't upset her and confided she was once so angry when rejected by a lover that she purchased a contract on him. That sounds pretty vicious but as a child and even now, I considered her life full of glamour and fantasize myself as her daughter.

To me, it was romantic to watch her showered with money and jewelry by wealthy men. Indirectly I also benefited; she paid for various classes from ballet to language instruction. I was raised as a princess; sent to an elite private school, private camps and summers in Switzerland. So there I was, a girl from a lower middle class family living like a rich girl. Can you envision a Flatbush kid, off to a camp in Switzerland and there at thirteen having her first love affair. Incredible but that is how it was. I had a fairy tale childhood; while the neighborhood kids were attending summer camps or going to the Catskills, I would attend elite camps or spend time with my aunt at her country club.

I lived a divided life which is not surprising. I was raised in fact by two women with different values and life styles. There were two messages; one from my profligate aunt and the other from a strict mother with an emphasis on education. At just sixteen, I was accepted by Barnard. By this time my aunt no longer could pay for school and through my own merits received a scholarship. In the second year, I transferred to Harvard, received a BA and much later a Masters in art history. Sometime in between, I attended the Sorbonne. During this phase, my life was subdued. I stayed alone and rarely associated with men. I was a proper young lady, studious and disciplined. This eventually ended.

A Story Out of Cinderella

It was difficult to be at the Sorbonne and live on a monthly allowance of two hundred dollars. Then as now, Paris was expensive and I was reluctant to press my family for funds. My solution seemed simple; I joined an escort service which was connected to the Hilton. I was innocent and naively believed an escort was kind of a date to accompany men to the theatre and to dinner. I quickly wised up when guys offered me extra money to sleep with them. They would give me two hundred dollars, sometimes three hundred. That was a lot of money to me. I knew a couple of hundred could go a long way and since it was so easy, I got into the life.

In a way, I began to live like the girl in Cabaret, except this was not Berlin in the 20's but Paris in the eighties. I felt totally free, often leaving Paris to hitch around the country side. One day, this wealthy guy, a count, picked me up on the road. I was on my way to Austria and he suggested we travel together. We arrived at a lovely hotel and although I refused to accept his invitation to share a room., he paid. It was fine with him and at that moment a kiss was sufficient. After settling in, he invited me to joint him at the casino. Naturally I was excited and my adult, fairy tale began.

I was only twenty, under the age limit, but because he knew the right people and flashed a lot of money, I was able to stay. It turned out to be a bonanza for him and a surprise to me. I found that I had a unique ability to select the right color or even number. Right off the top of my head, I would free associate; he won and kept on winning. He would tell me that I was his good, luck piece. Later when I returned to Paris, we kept in contact and he would invite me to join him at various gambling joints. There was nothing sexual about it; strictly about money. Unfortunately he left town and my savings ran out. It then seemed logical to me to return to the Hilton, escort gig. With the money earned there, I purchased lovely clothes, frequented fine restaurants and traveled a bit. I was living a pretty good life but nothing compared to the life style with my future husband.

Our meeting was serendipity. I was hitching on the road to Munich, intending to attend an opera festival. He simply gave me a lift and that seemed the end of it. Dropping me off in Munich, I thanked him and never expected to meet him again. Later when I returned to Paris, the escort service phoned and the prospective customer was the same person. We renewed our acquaintance, had a brief love affair and I was invited to be his guest at the Hilton. Life was fantastic; he gave me carte blanche permission to invite school friends to party. There seemed to be no limit to his generosity. He was a fantastic guy, coming from an old, established, rich family, but he was wealthy in his own right. He was trained as a geologist and developed oil fields. He was rolling in dough.

We soon became engaged which gave me a certain legitimacy. My story was that of Cinderella, from poverty to riches. When Jean was away which was often, I invited my friends to nightclubs, where I would order champagne, caviar and charge everything to him. He was relaxed about it, explaining it was best that I amuse myself while he was traveling. He believed I would stay out of trouble if I was occupied.

He invited me to join him in Africa and though I was just twenty and he thirty-two, we married there. After we returned to France, he bought me a Porsche and we drove to our new home; a lovely chateau in the South of France. It seemed like a fairy tale.

The bloom soon faded. Though we lived together for seven months, I only saw him for three weeks because of his business responsibilities. I invited my Parisian friends but they grew tired of the long trip. Our problem was the difference in expectations. I loved the notion of living my own life but he believed that once we were married, I should take the traditional path; supervise the house, have children and exist as a conventional couple. To me it was a drag. I was so lonely that one day I jumped into the Porsche, sped back to Paris and left it parked at the airport with the keys in it. I never heard from him again. I believe the rights to that chateau are probably still mine since we purchased it in both our names. We never divorced and I am still married according to the law. In truth, I have never divorced any of my husbands and I guess I could be considered a bigamist.

A Drug Smuggler

The time between my French escapades and until now, has been one adventure after another. All of it was great fun, although it was mostly financed by smuggling and soft, drug dealing.

Prior to starting my next adventure, I entered into a fiasco of a marriage that was doomed from the start. The man was brilliant and fascinating but there was one problem; he was a confirmed homosexual. I don't know why we married; probably we were too stoned to know better. He kept inviting male lovers into the home and after five months, it got to me and I left.

After that, I needed a break so I traveled to Israel and worked on a kibbutz. While there, my passport and money was stolen. Because I couldn't present proof of identity the American embassy was not helpful. No money, no passport, but as always, I adapted. I traveled to Jerusalem and found work as a bar maid. The job was pleasant and I enjoyed the company of the Arab men who hung around.

Even though I refused to sleep with them, they were happy to converse with an attractive, young woman. The owner was pleasant and respectful and eventually invited me to join him in smuggling hash from Jordan. The set up was like a movie. At that time, an Arab woman accompanied by her husband was not asked to show identification when traveling across the border. I transformed myself into a female, kind of a Lawrence of Arabia, dressed in a veil. We would meet our drug connection in Jordan. I would hide the hash under my clothes. At first my heart wildly beat but after a few trips across the border, it seemed as easy as taking candy from a baby. After twelve trips, I saved up a few thousand dollars. When my birth certificate finally arrived from the states, I obtained a passport and returned home with a small stake.

Back in Brooklyn, I tried a new gig, transporting pot from coast to coast. Learning from my Israeli experience, I again dressed in a disguise. At one time I had worked as a lab technician and decided to wear a lab uniform while carrying the stuff. The outfit helped me convince the airport officials that I had pressing medical work and they gave me priority through the line. I flew Friday nights, pick up as much as twenty kilos on the West Coast, stuff it into my suitcase and return the following day. With all the money made, I lived the high life; spending it on clothes, cars and travel. If things were slow, I would get help from a surgeon friend who would give me samples of "ups" and "downs" to sell. This in fact was a side line, selling small quantities to college kids. I did it for small change which was not risky. During this period my real, abiding interest was study and classes. With the arrival of summer break, the urge to travel captured me.

North Africa, particularly Morocco, was a place that I really enjoyed. It always seemed mysterious. One summer, accompanied by a French girl, I hitched into the desert. It was easy to find a ride but in the middle of the desert, the driver told us to "put out or get out". We made our choice to take our chances on the road. Fortunately by evening we were picked by another Moroccan who drove us to his home. It was weird because he lived in the middle of nowhere with a Norwegian wife who was desperate for company. We stayed there for a short period and then he proposed a deal. He said, "look, I have access to coke and I would like you to smuggle it into England". He promised customs would not be a problem because of contacts. Since I love risk and the high life, the deal was accepted.

The coke was placed in a Johnson's talcum, powder bottle. Passing through customs, the agent demanded to look into our luggage. I realized the guy had "bullshitted" us about special contact but there was nothing I could do. The agent opened the bottle and sneezed. The coke spilt onto the platform desk. I felt like shitting in my pants when he began to taste it. Amazingly, he didn't notice anything and let us through; Allah was with me then. Eventually we found our connection in London but much of the coke had crystallized and hardly any money was made.

After this episode, I decide it was stupid to be a courier. I felt it was time for me to make big money by becoming a wholesaler. I returned to North Africa and in Tunisia I purchased hash for six thousand dollars. I figured that if I sold it in the states, I stood to make fifty thousand dollars. I made it back to Paris without any trouble. I looked so young and innocent that customs didn't pose a problem.

Since the odor disguised the smell, my idea was to pack the hash in coffee bags. I planned to forward the "coffee" to a contact in Nebraska because I assumed customs would be less suspicious of a package mailed from Paris to Nebraska. I then flew back to the states and made my way there. I picked up the hash but was disappointed big time. I didn't realize that it would become wet when I originally wrapped the hash in moist plastic. It was suggested that I dry it in the oven. The process ended as a comedy of errors. Because it was excessively dried, the weight significantly diminished. Then I attempted to increase the weight by adding other substances. By this time, the hash developed fungi and it was terrible. I hoped the college kids would be gullible but it was such poor quality that nobody would touch it. I dumped the batch and took the loss.

"Selling My Body"

Obviously I was an amateur and not very good at the drug thing. Sure I made money but it would slip through my fingers or I would make a bad deal and end up with nothing. I later tried sell some of the coke but realized that between what I snorted and offered to friends, there was no money to be made. I then decided to return to the old tried and simple profession; selling my body.

It was easy to begin. I joined a massage parlor which in fact was a whore house. It was in a dismal apartment on the Upper East Side of Manhattan. Initially it seemed ideal because it gave me the time to continue my studies and I enjoyed hanging out with the "girls". Unfortunately, most of them were into drugs and supported their habit this way. At the evening's end we would socialize in after hour clubs which were usually frequented by black pimps and low life criminals. Some of the girls were groupies. They hung around rock groups and while the men were on tour, would pass their time at the parlor to pick up extra bread. I guess the common denominator for all of us was really drugs but underneath that was just "emptiness". We certainly weren't there for sex. The "Johns" were just things and to make it through the day, we would have to disengage and cut off all feelings.

I hate to say this, being Jewish, but the worst clients were the Hassidic men. They pretend to be holy but physically stunk with their dirty clothes and non-bathed bodies. I couldn't understand how they were not suppose to look at a strange woman and yet would come to the parlor to get their rocks off. The place began to get to me and I soon found myself shooting up with the other girls. I wasn't hooked on heroin but I was deeper into it then ever before. I estimated that in six months I made fifty-six thousand dollars, but because of the drugs, I had little to show for it.

My Long Island customers urged that I set up my own business out there. I was fed up with the parlor so I took the suggestion and rented a small place in Great Neck; an affluent community. I really started cleaning up but the isolation was worse then the New York gig. I found that I was not only going down on the "Johns" but almost any man I wanted something from. To get a free pizza, I would do it for the guy at the pizza store. In place of a tip I would go down on the delivery boy. I would do it for liquor, groceries; you name it. I was giving blow jobs like it was no tomorrow. I was out of control and part of me knew it.

Being Crazy and on Welfare

Living as a hooker took its toll. Simultaneously, I was working for my doctorate in art history but I was depressed and could barely study. I felt so empty that one day I stopped in my tracks and abandoned the house; leaving all my clothes and everything. I felt the possessions were not mine; they represented an ugly side of my life. I was desperate to change and moved to another residence. I then applied for welfare on the basis of a psychiatric history. You see, in the past I had been diagnosed as a borderline personality. Given a classification, "aid to the disabled", I received welfare for several years.

Of course, leaving the life of a dealer and prostitute didn't mean that I stopped enjoying sex and drugs. I got into Quaaludes which really stimulated my sexual appetite. Soon I started organizing sex orgies; not for money but just for plain fun. I would meet people at parties and invite them to my own special, Friday, night happening. We would all down some Quaaludes, get off and then do our thing. Sometimes it involved group "S&M" but nothing too dangerous. Most of those involved were educated professionals who seemed to really need this type of wild release.

One might wonder why the hell did I need Quaaludes to indulge in a sex orgy? It is just that this drug helped me feel uninhibited. Despite the fact that a psychiatrist diagnosed me as a sociopath, I do have a conscience; maybe not as much as the average person but it does put a damper on me.

I ended the orgies after a horrible event; a young doctor had a heart attack when fucking with me. While waiting for the ambulance, I was frightened, thinking "my god he is going to drop dead right here". After that, my friends would tease, I must be "hot stuff".

Life was easier on welfare. I no longer had to work full time as a prostitute though I continued with a few, well heeled clients. The amazing thing about manipulating the welfare system, I could travel to Europe, even go on to the Peace Corp in Micronesia and continued to receive money. My sister helped, picking up the checks from my mailbox. In fact, I probably would still be on welfare if they hadn't received an anonymous letter that gave the "ball game" away. Since my sister signed the checks it was considered forgery and the FBI was involved. They must have considered it small time; she was fined $2,500 and I was simply cut off.

During those years, it was easy to play the system. My selling point was that, "I was too crazy too work". The reality was I could work, but I disliked the idea of any authority telling me what to do. A doctor's report further confirmed my "nuttiness", emphasizing a tendency to hallucinate. The amusing fact is that I had been getting visions and flashes since the age of fourteen but this has never hindered me. Lasting for a few seconds, I am accustomed to them. Sometimes I hear voices that tell me to visit a certain place. Once I followed up the suggestion and actually found a new boyfriend. I consider myself psychic but some professionals label it schizophrenia. An example of my psychic powers is the consistency of my winning suggestions at the casino. I don't recall ever having frightening visions and sometimes I even receive excellent advice. My deceased grandmother tells me nice things and offers help. She will ask if I am happy and suggest how best to take care of myself. At times when driving, I will have hallucinations of people on the road, though part of me knows they are just visions. Frequently there is a particular guy that shows himself. He looks like a character out of a comic book, crosses the road and tips his hat. I am aware it is only a hallucination and will continue to drive. These visions might seem weird but by helping me get money from welfare, they were a blessing.

Going Straight

Though I have been classified both as a sociopath and schizoid personality, deep down I longed for a conventional, family life. Of course this meant finding a suitable husband. At first Bob was interested in my sister, who is quite square. I must admit that I stole him from her. The first time when we privately met, while kissing him I transferred a Quaalude into his mouth. I planned to hook him by inviting him on a trip to Europe. Much to my surprise he accepted the offer. I was open with him, revealing my jaded past and despite the fact that he was five years younger, he asked to marry me. Both of us had lived on the edge and in a basic way we were not that different. Sexually we were wild and neither of us had a problem with the notion of an open marriage.

I know it might sound weird but Bob was an ordained rabbi and also part of a coke ring. Bob's ring was busted and though he continued to deal, we were pissing it away and running short of money. We decided to split from the States. To change our lives we joined the Peace Corp. That sounds funny; two hustlers joining a "do good" organization but we were tired of our life and we wanted a fresh start.

Fortunately, the Peace Corp never found out about our illegal history and we were selected to go to Micronesia. Initially it was a close call. They tried to kick me out in the training period because of my "piss poor" attitude. I was considered too much of an individualist and "culturally insensitive". That label really got me angry because they wanted to control me and I wouldn't have it. The problem became worse while stationed on the island. The food was terrible. There was no fresh fruit or vegetables; one couldn't get fresh milk or eggs. The only half, decent thing to drink was a native, alcohol drink. To solve all of this, I arranged to have fresh food flown in at my expense. This didn't go well with the Peace Corp. Things really went downhill after I persuaded a few air force friends to take us to the other islands as part of our anniversary celebration. The authorities attempted to discourage anything I wanted to do. From my viewpoint, after the life I had been living, I wasn't going to be treated like a child. I would have just ended it but Bob enjoyed the life. We were both teaching and that was fine. Bob particularly loved life on this primitive island; it certainly was a change from Brooklyn. So when they tried to get rid of me, I struck back. I am quite articulate and wrote lengthy letters in my defense to our congressman and to governmental officials. I was successful and we remained for one year. We only left because I was pregnant.

Bob would have wanted us to stay but "wow" the idea of having a baby there was beyond belief. This was an island of only three hundred people and we were totally isolated from the outside world. I had lost twenty pounds because of the food and I was worried how the diet would affect the fetus. Also the typhoon season was really bad. The island was flat and there was no protection against the high winds. One literally had to tie oneself to a tree to keep from being blown into the sea. In fact, after our first typhoon, we learned a family lost a few kids who weren't properly tied down.

In some ways, we regretted leaving because it was kind of a tropical paradise. There was little work and the natives would just lounge around during the day, waiting for the U.S. government plane to fly in food. Bob thought it was weird they didn't even fish since he loved to scuba amongst the bountiful, marine life. There were no stores and thus little need for money. In a way, school was useless and ridiculous since there were no jobs to prepare for. It was unlikely they could leave because the adjustment would be too great. Few wore shoes, so you can imagine them arriving in California wearing flimsy clothes and no shoes. They had no practical idea about the economics of money and if they ate in a restaurant, they would expect to be fed for free. In their culture, nobody eats alone and no one charges for food. Furthermore, accustomed to a flat island, they probably couldn't deal with heights such as a hi- rise.

End of the Journey

Much to the satisfaction of the Peace Coup, we departed to England via Asia. Along the way, we visited villages in Northern Thailand which adjoins the Golden Triangle. If one was into drugs, this was heaven. In our room, they would accommodate us with a vase full of hash and grass. I noticed six year old kids smoking opium. It was weird, when we were offered a kilo of hash for ten dollars and refused, the villager believed we were bargaining and reduced the price to five dollars. Because I was pregnant, I refrained but Bob went on a fling with opium, remaining stoned most of the time we were there. Later in England, I bragged to a friend about the scene and he became so excited about the possibilities that he traveled there and shipped back over five hundred pounds of hash. He marked the boxes as ginseng. Unfortunately the British customs official was curious about the nature of ginseng and opened the box. The poor bastard ended in jail. Somehow both of us were lucky and avoided the consequences of our smuggling or pushing.

Living in England was marvelous. I was nine months pregnant when we arrived and Gail, my daughter, was born healthy and everything worked out fine. I received another degree; a MSW and found work in a hospital. Bob, used his drug expertise, "ha", to get a position as a drug detail man. We were able to land jobs without papers, because we each claimed the other as an English subject. Fortunately, the British were trusting and never checked on us. Life was mellow and we even saved sufficient money to purchase a lovely condo. Unfortunately, Bob's father took ill and we returned to the states. We still ended up on top. His father was a tailor and over the years, saved every cent he made. Prior to his death, he turned over to Bob, his life savings; a quarter million dollars in cash.

At this point in our lives, we intend to find a lovely place to settle and peacefully raise our daughter. Am I a good mother? Who knows; when she is not around I don't think of my daughter, though of course, I love her. My intention is to hire an au pair and work. I know both of us will stay straight because we have enough to live the good life. Looking back, I have no regrets, except that I wished I had even more adventures.

Postscript

Several years later, I encountered a mutual friend who informed me that the couple settled in San Francisco. Barbara had two children and projected herself as a middle class matron devoted to her kids. She and her husband lived a straight and legitimate life. Unfortunately, they were constantly at odds and in the end, they fought each other in a vicious divorce. From her perspective, the issue was a need for more spending money and from his; her behavior as an irresponsible mother.

3

"I Forgot How to Laugh"

The heart of East Harlem is located between 96th and 116th street bordered on the East by the East River and the West by Central Park. It is predominately Latin, mixed with a Afro-American and a small, aging Italian community. It could be classified as a Latin ghetto, consisting of Puerto Ricans, Dominicans and other Hispanic groups. It is a self-contained barrio, reflecting a culture of "bodegas", domino players hanging out, salsa music blaring and a lively street world. A traveling tourist might think he is in the third world or a Latin American village. He would be struck by the large number of "street people" that crowd the corners and lurk from doorways morning through the night. If one is in a car, the typical reaction would be to close the windows, lock the doors and try to ignore this foreign and seemingly threatening world. Not only is the value system alien but even the sense of time. The "street people" out there might seem dangerous because they seem so different. Such a perspective is not far from the truth for many in this ghetto, the lives are scared by violence and dysfunction.

This story is about Pablo and Vivian, a dysfunctional Romeo and Juliet tale. To an outsider they might be discounted as typical "street people" and thus invisible. But their tale offers a different picture; they are not just "creatures from the deep", but oppressed, vulnerable victims who live out a "no-exit" existence. It is also a story of love contaminated by violence, between a middle aged, Puerto Rican man who is entrapped by concepts of "machismo" and a sixteen year old, frightened, abandoned, Afro-American teenager.

Growing up to Hate

Pablo, is in his early forties, has light brown skin, salt and pepper hair and a lined face. He is short but has a wiry, tough quality about him and carries himself like a bantam weight fighter. At times he is quite pleasant but is mercurial and when upset can be menacing.

I never met my father because I was a product of a one night stand back in PR (Puerto Rico). I never got over that early feeling of being a "bastard" and it didn't help when I was "put down" with that word. I believe this is one of the reasons I have been angry and destructive for most of my life. Still, I have this yearning to meet the old man or at least to know something about him. Not knowing leaves me with an empty feeling.

My mother raised me until the age of six but when she hooked up with this guy who I guess, would be considered my stepfather, she lost herself. She loved him so much that I was forgotten and bounced around various homes. She later had a girl by him and he really loved the kid. As for me, he would always find an excuse to kick me around; the message was obvious, I wasn't welcome.

I recall an incident that to this day causes me pain. I was only seven and secretly took pocket money from his pants. With a few friends, I went to the store and purchased toys. My intentions were innocent; to buy gifts for all of us. I didn't even understand what I was spending. I didn't consider it stealing but I sensed that I had done something wrong. I hid on the top steps, near the roof. He must have been looking for me because when he noticed, he strode two stairs at time, grabbed me and dragged me into the house. I was petrified as I watched him roll up a newspaper and light a match. He turned me over on my stomach, sat on my back and took off my shoes. He then pinned me down while he burnt my feet.

My mother said nothing. After, she helped me to my little bed, which pathetically was still a crib. To this day, I clearly can see her crying while using a needle to puncture the blisters to take out the water.

After this incident, I forgot how to laugh. I no longer wanted to learn in school and became what was called, a trouble maker. I felt nobody cared, so nothing mattered. All I could feel was just hate. I hated real hard.

Foster Homes

Not wanted at home, I lived a life as a foster child. There it was a life of roaming and fighting. Both worlds were no bargain. If I was placed with a Black couple, I would end up in a Black neighborhood. After school, I usually had to fight my way home because the Black kids considered me "white". When I was with white foster parents, the reverse would happen. I'd have to fight the White kids who considered me black because of my brown skin. I was called a "spick". That didn't really matters since we called each other names. Italians would be "guineas"; Irish, were known as "micks", Blacks were called "niggers". We were just one great, dirty soup.

While I was transferred to many homes, there was one that stood out. The foster parent was an undertaker and went out of his way to teach me embalming. When the cadavers were transferred from Bellevue, I'd help out, holding a basin while blood was drawn. Later I was taught how to cut under the armpits to drain the body. I learned how to stick cotton in the cadaver's nose and underneath the eyelids and even how to inject the embalming fluid. I cleaned the body of feces and urine because when a person dies, he looses bladder and bowel control. I recall watching an autopsy and how the body opened like a book so that one can see the inside. I remember carrying the cadaver after the autopsy was completed. I learned a lot. I was only thirteen.

While some homes were fine, others terrible; it really didn't matter. I would continually attempt to run away back home because I wanted to with my mother. I was always forcefully sent back. Inside, I felt mean and angry and I hated everybody and everything. Even with the funeral director, who probably loved me in his own way, I destroyed what was good. I stole two hundred dollars from him and because the agency felt I was uncontrollable, I was brought before the court. It was decided that I was unmanageable and I was sent away to Warwick reformatory.

Training to be a Punching Bag

Before I entered the reform school, they promised I would learn a trade. They suggested that I would be given a chance to change my life around. I learned a whole lot there; to hate, even more.

I was often caught fighting. You couldn't even talk to me because I would swing out in response. Then as now, people couldn't understand what was with me because it seemed I was always looking to hurt somebody. Yeah, I carried a lot of angry baggage, but they educating me even more to severely hurt others and of course, they hurt me a lot.

I escaped twice. The first time I made it across the George Washington Bridge intending to find my mother. The state police caught up with me and brought me back. Mr. H., who was in charge of caring for the cattle and pigs, was the disciplinarian. He was prepared for me; putting on leather gloves, he used me for a punching bag. After the beating, I was locked up for a week. A week later I was allowed to return to the classroom. I was expected to follow orders and learn. It didn't work because school was of no interest to me. I didn't want to know none of that stuff. I was just too full of rage.

Fighting Back

While I was put away, my mother broke up with my stepfather. Today, in my heart I forgive him, but then it was a different story. On the day they cut me loose from Warwick, I returned home and unfortunately he was visiting when I arrived. I was young, strong and I knew how to handle myself. When I noticed him in the living room, I went wild; grabbing him, I tried to throw him out of the window. Both my mother and sister screamed for me to stop. I wanted revenge; but because of them, I pulled him back from the edge.

He didn't come around after that but he continued to support my mother and sister. Right now I am crying inside, thinking that if I had been his natural son, he would have been a damn good father as he was to my stepsister. I wanted somebody and there was nobody.

My mother allowed me to remain though I was difficult. Perhaps she was guilty because of the way she had pushed me out when I was just a young kid. I tried to explain to her my hurt and what it was doing to me. I told her that I loved her, despite everything, and I hoped to remain with her.

After a quiet spell, I got hooked up with a gang, fighting in the streets and all that kind of garbage. I ended up in jail for stealing one lousy bottle of milk. We had stayed up all night, smoking pot and a neighbor complained to the police and from her window, fingered me. The police got me for the bottle of milk. I was real nasty to them and that didn't help matters. They took me into a back room of the station and gave me a good ass whipping.

I did two weeks for that bottle in the Tombs. It was the first time I went to an adult jail. The guards would order you to stand in line and even if your hand was out of line, they would give it a good whack. If you attempted to wear a hat, cocking it to the side for example, to teach you respect they would knock you down and kick you in the head. I learned where there are mean people, you have to be fierce and know how to fight back.

Discharged and back on the streets, I hung out on 113th Street and Madison Avenue with a pretty rough, older crowd. They enjoyed ripping people off. I was still considered a kid and they would urge me to provoke fights with bigger guys. Then the older guys from the gang would jump the victim; beating and stealing him blind. I did all that kind of garbage but now, I am sorry about it.

Revenge and the Family

No matter what was happening to me, I continued to remain close to my mother and sister. Even when I was married, I regularly visited. I recalled once caring for my mother who was ill from a job which was stuffing animals with cotton. The problem was that the cotton would float up into her nose and make her dizzy. While there, my sister arrived, upset from a fierce argument with her husband. I exploded when I heard that he had beaten her up. Returning to their home, I beat his brains out. Part of me knew it was wrong; not to interfere with their marriage, but I couldn't help myself. All I knew was he was causing pain to one of the two people I loved. I would have died for either of them. Today, it might have been different, knowing there is always matrimonial strife; at times a man hits his wife or a wife fights with her husband. All I could think of was someone hurt my sister and I was going to make him pay. I realize now that my crazy reaction was due to a demon inside of me. It reminded me of the times that my stepfather would return home late at night, drunk, and beat my mother. Listening to the screams, I would cry myself to sleep.

This demon inside me was beyond anger, it included suspicion and jealousy. When drunk, I would fantasize how women cheated on their husbands while they were out working during the day. I recall as a young kid, I watched my babysitter who was married make love to another man. Even worse, while my stepfather was at work I caught my mother with another man; no wonder I mistrust women.

When I was married, the mistrust was so intense, that if my wife was delayed returning home, I would knock her down. I just assumed she was with somebody else. I know I gave her a hard time; a real, rough time, especially after drinking. Entering the house, I would immediately think she was with somebody else. I would call her all sought of names; "tramp", "bitch", whore". Of course she couldn't understand that it was the demon inside of me that was creating this distrust. She tried to be a good wife but it was too much for her.

One day, after spending time in the street smoking pot, I arrived home late. I forgot it was my son's birthday because I was "high". The party was over. My children, a body and a girl were asleep in their bedroom in a bunk bed. On the bottom bunk was my wife was having sex with my best friend. The fire within me exploded. I picked him up; punched him around and then heaved him out the window. Then I tried to kill her. Grabbing her hair, I beat her but she finally broke away, leaving me with a mass of hair in my hand. I ran after her as she fled screaming and naked through the building's hallway. Fortunately a neighbor pulled my wife into her apartment for safety. Since I liked that neighbor and out of respect, I didn't break the door down and kill my wife. I returned to my apartment and I learned from my son that he was told "mommy would beat them if they said anything". The kids watched through the curtain while those two made love. I returned to the neighbor with the kids and yelled, "take the kids, I am leaving". I was sobbing as I ran down the stairs. I glanced up and when I saw her take the kids inside, my heart split open. I stopped off at a bar. Some guy said something to me and I simply stabbed him in the chest. I can't explain why.

I decided to leave the neighborhood and moved into a furnished room in the Bronx. I was making good money then; dealing in pot and getting into different things. Meanwhile my wife remained in contact with my mother, regularly visiting on Sundays. Alone in a furnished room, I thought of my babies and would sob myself to sleep. One Sunday I met my wife and persuaded her to go out to a restaurant. We talked things over and because of the kids, decided to reconcile. I tried to forgive her but I couldn't forget she was unfaithful. Those thoughts wouldn't leave me.

Becoming a Junkie

Eventually I got a straight job. I was a good worker but I met a hard core druggie at work. He invited me up to his house and I noticed his "works" on the bed. He got off and then I told him I wanted some. He begged me not to, but I was confident I wouldn't get hooked. The dose was small but it was too strong. I jumped around and unable to catch my breath; like receiving ether, I felt I was going under. Unable to catch my breath, heart racing, I just wanted to run. I grabbed the door to get outside but yet, I could hardly move. I made it into the street and when I hit the fresh air, it seemed that my head split straight down the middle and all the wind was flowing inside my brain.

That night I approached my wife for sex. I lasted almost eleven hours, keeping an erection, feeling like an animal yet I couldn't come. My wife could hardly get out of bed; she was wasted. The following day, I again returned to the junkie's house. Thank god for my big veins, they were easy to get to and weren't destroyed like most of my addict friends. I borrowed his needle, along with a dropper, hooked my veins with a rubber band and prepared for the fix. I learned quickly and became good at it.

My body shrunk and both my wife and mother remarked I was becoming thin. One morning before "getting off", I forgot to lock the bathroom door. I just shot up and my wife burst in; her mouth dropped and she let out a scream "oh my God, not you too" (her brother was also a junkie). I blamed her, replying "that's what you wanted, an addict; that is the only way you can be sexually satisfied...love wasn't enough...you need to be sexually satisfied and so long as I use this drug, I can do it...I'll more then satisfy you this way". Since she was savvy about heroin addiction, she understood there was nothing that could be done at that point.

I spent most of my money on dope and even borrowed from other people. It affected my life on the job. Before the addiction, my boss developed a real liking for me. Frequently he would invite me to his house on weekends and we worked on his projects. He soon noticed my slowing down and demanded to know the reason. Because he was good to me and I respected him, I opened up. He offered to help, suggesting the addict hospital in Lexington, Kentucky. When I was accepted there, as token of trust, he gave me two hundred dollars and his watch. I spent the money on dope, kept the watch and never returned to the job.

My wife couldn't take it anymore and I don't blame her. She was concerned that my habit would affect the kids. We still had lots of sex and as a result; a baby girl. One day, I cursed her out because she refused to help me out with more money. I was in bed, sick, because I couldn't afford a fix. She stared out the window, crying and begging me to straighten up. I was shivering and angry. I blamed her for my habit, reminding her of the time she slept with a friend. I accused her of sleeping around, yelling, "there is no woman in the world I can trust; there is none, you are all the same". She split with the kids and I was alone again.

I stumbled down into the street and stole to pay for my next fix. I continued to return home, checking and hoping she would return. Finally after a week, she showed up. She wouldn't let me back into the apartment, despite my banging and raging at the door. Finally she got an order of protection from Family Court demanding I keep away or be arrested. At our final meeting, she told me she wanted a divorce. I was furious, responding "go ahead and get it" and then with my usual suspiciousness, accused her of finding someone else.

A few months after the separation, I learned that an addict acquaintance was having sex with her. I tracked him down and beat him to a pulp. I was getting real demoralized. It got so bad I stopped visiting the kids. I lived out on the streets, in basements or deserted apartments. I began to believe that the kids were better off without me. When I later learned she married a good guy, I was relieved. My son told me this guy was kind to them and I felt happy for them.

Life was a revolving door, in and out of jail, stealing to pay for the dope and getting busted. I was also lonely and by a miracle met up with a wonderful innocent young girl. It happened in the Midwest at a Christian oriented place where I was sent to kick the habit. I made a good initial impression and after rehab they even sent me to a bible institute to train to become a minister. It was a three year program and I actually managed to make it through two years. There I gave her a story about my love for her, knowing it was a lot of bullshit; but I didn't care. I no longer wanted to be alone and I needed sex. I took her virginity. She was a good woman. Because she always came through, I learned to trust her but due to the dope, this gift from heaven was lost to me. I dropped the bible program and was out there again looking for the next fix. Although we took a furnished room together, I went back to my old habits and ended up in jail. She rented an apartment nearby and never missed a visit. She told me, she would always be there for me. I recall a picture she sent of her cat, Tulip and on the back wrote, she loved me very much. Out of jail, I couldn't escape my addiction. Desperate for money, she wired her mother to prevent me from stealing. She would return home from work, find me nodding, and still prepare supper. I knew she was suffering. Finally she begged me to let her go; "Pablo I can't compete with the drugs". She left to be with her mother and eventually found another guy. She still wanted to keep in touch but I told her "don't write no more because it would be unfair to the guy". In my mind, I didn't want her to be that kind of woman. I wanted to imagine her as pure and good. I had other women, but she was the only one I ever really trusted.

From a Fix to a Drink

Finally I left dope but choose a different bag which was equally bad or maybe worse; I became an alcoholic. The first time I attempted to kick this habit in a detox unit, I got the horrors; seeing thing and shaking like crazy. I promised myself, to never drink again. Unfortunately after discharge, I met up with a friend and accepting an invitation to join him with a bottle. It started again. Once hooked on alcohol, it was a hell of a thing to break away from. It seemed like a drink was always available but nobody could provide a plate of food.

When you get drunk, you are a fool; you get into all kinds of trouble. While on drugs, nothing happened to me, but with alcohol, I was like an idiot. I got piped in the head; got my wrists busted with a baseball bat and got stabbed. After a night of drinking I would be out there at 9:00 AM, waiting for the liquor store to open. Everyday I was boozed up, even on Sunday. It was a hell of a habit to break.

Violence and Love

In the midst of a drinking spree I met this young chic, Vivian. One of my pals told me of this skinny, 16 year old girl who was out there on the street and guys were taking advantage of her. He urged me to put her under my wing; give her place to sleep and get her some food because she was going hungry. I thought, "shit, I don't even know what she looks like" but I was drunk and agreed. The truth was I was tired of being lonely. As soon as I asked her to join me, without any questions, she agreed.

The mind is strange because no sooner was she with me that I started thinking of the stories about her being fucked by everybody. I couldn't help but conclude she was a tramp. I intended her to be a one night stand because the thoughts of sluts and women using me, gets me bent out of shape. When she got to my place, the first thing I did was beat her. Maybe I am sadistic. I don't know.

The following morning I kicked her out and joined my drinking friends. One of the guys propositioned her in the street and she disappeared with him for the night. The following morning on the way from the liquor, I noticed them coming toward me.

I wasn't going to pay her no mind but the guy came over to me. He then spoke in Spanish so she wouldn't understand, "here man, take this woman. I don't want her. On second thought, you should cut her loose. She ain't into nothing. She don't know how to do nothing right. She's just something that you throw away; throw your waste into her when you want relief. Anybody can have her; all they have to do is ask".

I stared at her and she looked back with sorrowful eyes. I already drank a pint of Smirnoff but it didn't kill the pity. "Come on back", I said and took her home.

Vivian knew nothing about the kitchen, except to open a can so I taught her basics, like how to make rice and beans. Little by little we made contact. Still she kept resisting me. I didn't understand the reason but I got to feel real sorry for her. I was sure I didn't want her to again end up on the street. Like my friend had said, "they were using her for a waste can". Even with my protection, they would grab her and sometimes I would fight to keep the vultures away. They thought she was a bum because she wore mini skirts. They called her a "dizzy broad" and were always coming on to her. Finally, I moved us from the neighborhood. I no longer could take the flack and feared I would do something real mean and destructive.

Mistrust

One evening, returning home late, I knocked but there was no answer. I thought she was asleep, and pounded real hard and screamed out for about five minutes, "where the hell are you?" I saw her on the floor above and demanded she come down. She turned the other way and walked away. I ran up and noticed a friend's door open.

She was sitting on a chair in the corner and he was in bed under the blanket but his clothes were lying by his side. At first I just stared at her, thinking, "you can't stop her; she must be over sexed because she always wants to make it with anybody". I asked "what was going on?" She was nervous and explained "because you were gone so long I got worried, thinking something happened. Then I met your friend. He took me by the arm to his room, to talk to me". I then quizzed her, asking, "how come you couldn't talk in the lobby?" I began to get angry, telling her "no one forced you to go to this guy's room". She started shaking. Her voice was low as she told me, "I didn't get in bed with him or do anything". I kept quiet, not believing her because it reminded me when I walked in on my wife with a guy. Still I stayed with her, taking as much care of her as I could. But I continued to drink and drink like there was no tomorrow.

A few months later she told me she was pregnant and I wondered, by whom? She claimed it was me. "Oh yeah, I believe that", I replied. When she told me a second time, I yelled, "you're full of shit; you know you're full of shit. No one gives a damm for you and so you figure if you get hung up with a kid, nobody will care, except for me". After that, I put her through a whole lot of changes, treating her real mean. At times I would give her the silent treatment and just stare at her while she talked.She would have tantrums, break things and then beg me to believe her.

Because of the yelling and noise, they threw us out of that flea ridden hotel. At that point, I could have returned to my mother's home and just forget her but she had nobody. I knew I couldn't leave her alone like that. We slept in an abandoned apartment in a deserted building, freezing half to death. It was winter and it was cold as hell. One time we were forced outdoors, sleeping on a park bench, with her head resting on my lap. We walked in the snow; in the rain. We went through a lot of hell.

While Vivian was in the hospital, I tried to approach her mother. I wanted her to understand that Vivian has love for her. That she should realize that Vivian was just a kid and young people do foolish things without thinking of the consequences. Her mother's heart remained closed. Since we were without a home, Vivian tried to return to her family. Her mother refused to forgive her and wouldn't even touch the baby. One evening and for no reason, she threw both of them out into the street. I knew something bad was going to happen because when I arrived with flowers, the mother threw them on the table as if they were nothing. I tried to act as a gentleman and remained quiet but the mother kept attacking and criticizing Vivian. Finally I couldn't stand it and warned the mother. I noticed her husband standing nearby and I was prepared for any kind of move. If they had hurt the baby or Vivian, I intended to kill everyone in that house and set fire to it. I mean that from the bottom of my heart.

Out on the street again, we know it is impossible to properly care for our baby. Today, we are still out in the cold, waiting for her and the baby to be placed in emergency housing. Meanwhile I am spent, having not slept for the last twenty four hours but I still believe things will improve. The most important thing is that I believe she wasn't lying; the baby was mine. I got the most beautiful baby in the world. She never lied; it was my baby. I'll tell it to the whole world, "I am proud to have this baby". I know one thing; "God has never let me down and will not, now that I am again a father". The funny part about all of this, "I love this dizzy broad". She is clean now; nobody bothers or touches her. And if anybody tries, they got to kill me first. If those around us can't be friendly with her, ain't no way in the world they could ever receive my friendship. I vow that instead of hanging around with those bums, spending money on booze, the baby is going to get whatever I can give. I am going to be a good father and I know she will be a good mother because she loves this baby.

Vivian

If one needed to describe Vivian, the term "big" would be appropriate. She is close to six feet and of medium weight. She is a dark skin, Afro-American with strong Negroid features and while under eighteen, looks older. There is little of the innocence of a teenager in her expressions, yet when she discusses people she cares about, she radiates strong emotion and warmth.

Family

I like my name, Vivian. I was born in Harlem hospital seventeen years ago. As far back as I can remember I never believed my family loved me; this is why I am such a nervous person. I was always fighting with my sisters and brothers and if anything was broken, it was always me that was blamed. In fact, even if I didn't do it, I would take the blame.

My elder sister, who is now nineteen, never liked to be seen in public with me because she thought I was so ugly. I have a brother who is fifteen and two younger ones; six and five. These two I consider my baby brothers and I love them very much.

I have never seen my real father or at least I don't remember seeing him. When I would ask about him, my mother would tell me he was dead, but I really didn't believe her. I recalled a strange phone call where this man said he had a daughter name Vivian and that he wanted to see her. I told him, "this is Vivian" and he started crying and said he was my real father. He wanted to know if I was happy and how was my mother getting along. I wasn't happy but didn't tell him because I was afraid he might interfere with my family and then I would get blamed. I told him I would come to meet him but he said "no, never mind". He was still crying when he hung up the phone. I never told my mother because my stepfather was always there and I didn't want her to get worried or anything. I hurt for a long after that but I tried to hide it.

My problem was that I was always nervous and fidgety. I would pace around the house not knowing what to do with myself. When I was younger I had habit of rocking back and forth and my mother would yell, "stop acting like you are crazy." I wasn't crazy but people used to say that I acted like I was retarded or something. I knew I wasn't but it was hard since they kept labeling as if I was. On top of that, I was ugly or least that is what people would say and I began to believe them. People would treat me as if I was ugly, stupid or crazy. I would lend my sister everything I had and though she promised to return the items, she would never do it. I would be quiet, cry and wonder why people hated me and took advantage of my kindness.

Kicked Around

Not just with my family but friends, I was kicked around. Arriving late to school, I met my best friend who urged me to join her and a group that were hanging out in the hallway. I was scared and worried but I figured she was my friend and wouldn't let anybody hurt me. I was eleven and she was twelve but the others were older and into drugs. We all split from school and ended up on the roof of the friend's house. She and the others grab me and held me over the roof by my feet. They wanted money for dope and demanded that I get it. I was terrified and screamed, "I don't know where, please let me alone". I was crying but it didn't do any good. One of them pulled out a knife and warned, "shut up; we will keep on eye on you until you bring us money".

At that time I really believed my mother cared for me. When I returned home I kept quiet because I thought she would attack the girls or call the cops. I was so afraid that even if some of them went to jail, the others would try to kill us. I believed to protect my family there was no choice but to take my mom's money.

The next day I returned to school late because I was told to dress my brothers. The teacher was angry and pushed me in such a way that my nose started to bleed. I never even got to show him the "excuse" letter. I was just sitting there crying, listening to him yell, "Vivian, sit up and do your work". I was shivering inside, thinking of the money I stole for those girls.

Returning home, I heard my mother call out, she was "missing money". At first, she asked my sister and older brother about it. Then she approached me. I was afraid to tell her the truth, replying over and over, "no, I didn't take nothing". She grabbed an ironing board to beat me, screaming, "Vivian you're going to make me kill you".

The next day, I passed by those girls and they started following me. They demand that I steal ten dollars. I begged them, "please no, I can't do it". This time they threatened to stab me and because I was so frightened, I agreed. Again I stole from my mother, but only five dollars because I thought if it was ten, she would really hate me. I brought the money to them and later returned home. My mother was real mad, screaming, "Vivian, you took money from me". She never even asked why I was doing it but just loudly yelled which got me so nervous that all I could do was cry. I knew she was going to beat me bad, as she pulled off my clothes so that strap would really hurt. Completely naked, I ran downstairs to the landlady. My mother came after me, demanding that I return. I replied in a very low voice, "no, I am afraid" but I went back. She ordered me to sit on a chair and then she just threw a shoe which hit me in the eye. After that she gave me a good whipping; my body was badly bruised. At that point, it didn't matter; I no longer cared for my body; not even for myself. The next day, she ordered me to stay home, not because I was hurt but she feared that people would think badly of her for what she did. My mother went to work and I went to school anyway because I no longer cared. I believed not only nobody loved me but they all hated me.

I continued to steal and steal from my mother for those kids. I felt I was protecting mine and my mother's life. I didn't want her to get hurt because then all of us would end up in foster homes. Even then, I always wanted us to remain a whole family.

Escape into Madness

Because the beatings and threats were too much for me, I started disappearing from home. The cops would be called and I would be brought right back home. One day I ran away for a few days. I was living in the streets with a man that took dope though I refused to touch it. During this time, every man on the block was having sex with me; I didn't care. My thirteenth birthday arrived and went. Deep down, I wanted somebody who would care and love me.

When the cop found me, I was dirty and filthy. Accompanied by my mother, they brought me to Kings County hospital because they thought I was crazy. The doctors asked me all sought of questions and I ended up staying for a year. Later I was transferred to a larger hospital which seemed like a big island with no way out. My first night in the hospital, I dreamt that my mother killed me. Nightmares became a regular thing with me.

I really didn't want to see the psychiatrists because I believed nothing was really wrong with my head. In fact the psychiatrist agreed that I wasn't crazy but there was a problem with my mother and family. Yet they gave me lots of medicine which seemed to make my nerves worse.

I should add they gave all of us lots of medicine so we wouldn't create a disturbance but it didn't work. One night, a few of the girls came to my bed and slapping my face, woke me up. They demanded I join them in starting a riot. I first refused because I wanted to keep a good record and get out. Yet, I gave in because I had a need for friends. I broke forty windows with my hands, just so they would accept me. When it was over, they went to the nurse and accused me. At first, I could only stare at them and then I burst out crying. I felt betrayed.

The nurses gave me a needle to knock me out and put me in a strait jacket. I was so frightened but resisted. It took four aides a long time to control me but finally I got so tired and gave up; "go ahead, you are going to win anyway". They dumped into the isolation room which was like a cell with only a mattress; it was for real sick patients. I cried myself to sleep and during the night I had another nightmare that people were pushing drugs on me. The next day they released me to the ward and there I just stared at the walls. They broke my spirit.

The girls frequently picked on me. At time I tried to make believe I was crazy, hoping they would leave me alone. It didn't work because they were really crazy and didn't know the difference. Sometimes they would jump me in the bathroom. Once they attacked me with sticks, hitting my body and face, but I would say nothing; only cry.

Twice a month my mother would visit but it was irregular, using the excuse she was busy. I never wanted to take the money she offered because I believed she didn't love me and I felt worthless. The money never meant anything to me; all I wanted from her was love and some affection.

Even when I got a little money, say five dollars, the girls would be after me. They would search the room and of course would find it. They continually bugged me, "Vivian can we have it?" I knew if I refused, they would take it anyway so I would say, "yea go ahead", but I didn't mean it. I would get really angry, not say anything and go into my room and cry. There I would think to myself, "maybe I'm getting paid back for the money I stole from my mother".

Hard Life

Christmas was always sad for me. The presents I received from my mother and little brothers would be stolen by the girls on the ward. I felt bad because I had nothing to give my family. The first year at the hospital, I went home for Christmas but it no longer felt like home. After that, I rarely went back during the hol-idays. I felt like a stranger with my own family. I kept quiet, afraid to speak up. I wanted to cry but would wait until everyone was asleep and then quietly weep myself to sleep. I tried to please my mom by cleaning but it was no good; my mother didn't trust me. I no longer belonged anywhere; my mother didn't want me and this made me feel very bad.

It was a very hard life in the hospital but I remained because there was no where else to go. The girls would provoke disturbances and because I joined them, the aides strapped me in a straitjacket. Once in a struggle to get out, I almost smothered myself to death. Still some the nurses, treated me well and I appreciated it. There was a nurse who called me "peaches" and really liked me. She would keep me company during the night shift, bring me things to eat and try to protect me. Even with her help, everything I owned would be stolen and I can say "I never had anything for myself". Even my toothpaste was stolen or they would crush the tube. They would rip my clothes. They would grab my letters and throw it out the window. Finally it got to a point that I wanted to destroy everything I had. I, myself, would rip up the clothes, crush my toothpaste and give them all my things; knowing they would take them anyway.

I remember asking them, "do you want five dollars?" Then I would give it to them and walk away with tears in my eyes. I would tell them, "you can have any-thing I got because I know you'll then be my friends."

I was afraid of everything and everybody in this world. To escape I would hang out in the back yard of the hospital but it didn't do any good. During the winter, the girls would find me and push snow into my face. I was furious but I couldn't show it and as usual, cry. In the summer, they would find frogs and put them down my pants. I grew to hate the place and the people in it. I felt I wasn't crazy and didn't belong there and if I stayed I was going to loose my mind. I tried to run away and escaped three times but I was always caught.

One thing I loved was school. At first it was hard to be there because I was on too much medicine. I would get dizzy and fall. I was unable to eat, my blood wasn't right and I was weak. Finally they lowered the dosage enough so that I could get to the classroom. The girls were cruel there. When I would answer questions correctly or seem to get close to the teacher, the girls would get mad and call me "bitch". It seems all my life people used that name for me. I ask myself, "why"?' This confuses me because I feel that I have more love for people than anybody in this world. I really care for people. I don't like to hurt anyone because I know what it is to be hurt.

At the doctor's office, he would spend time with me and I enjoyed talking with him. One day he excused himself, explaining he had to give somebody a shot because they were upset. While he was out, I searched the office and stole two bottles of pills.

Later I showed the girls on the ward and they claimed it was urine pills and made a big joke of it and I felt they were laughing at me. I decided that I would play the joke on them. I notice on the bottom of the bottle, the label was "sleeping pills". I shared this with my friend, Hilda, whispering, "don't tell anybody, please, but I took sleeping pills". She cared for me, didn't want me to die and told the nurse. The nurse took me to the medical building where I slept it off for four days. It was strange that they didn't pump my stomach but though I didn't die, I felt like it. Later, they told me they tried to give me coffee and slapped my face but I didn't remember, perhaps because in a way I was already dead. While in that half alive-dead state, it seemed like my soul was floating away. I saw my mother and little brothers and drifting away. I said my "goodbyes". On the fifth day, I woke up and they told me if I had slept one more day, I would have died. I could think "I wished I succeeded". The nurse tried to comfort me and asked "why do you say a terrible thing like that?" She could never understand how the daily humiliations drove me to do something like that.

Fighting Back

While recovering, I helped the aides clean and make the beds. I noticed the old people couldn't care for themselves and whenever possible, helped them. The nurses tried to discourage me, but I liked to work and persisted, until they finally gave in. I was there for only three days but for me, it was the best time in the hospital. I met a pretty lady there; she had glasses and long, brown hair. She seemed to like me and I felt she understood and made me feel that I was a "person". When it was time to leave, I cried but she told me, "Vivian, don't be sad, be happy you are alive and you can always come to visit". I tried to explain that "I don't want to return to those kids because my mind is not crazy; I don't belong with them". She reassured me, "someday you'll be out of there and you will be happy; just wait and have patience". She was the one who encouraged me to stay alive.

I returned to the ward and they were waiting for me; five of them. Mollie, their leader, started joking and soon they were all laughing at me. She had a friend named Barbara, a lesbian, who also acted as a big shot. She was fat and dirty; real dirty. I couldn't stand her. Every time Barbara talked, she had to curse at you. The memory is so clear; the girls led by Mollie and Barbara, laughing and humiliating me. I turned to them, yelling, "I don't want to hear anymore of this shit. Leave me the hell alone; get out of my life". I told them that "I hated them and if any of them bothered me, I was ready to kill." They mocked me, "oh no, you won't; you can't kick no bodies ass". I finally got to a point where I couldn't take it, yelling "I am tired of your bull shit; all of you act like you own me". I ran to my room, slammed the door but they followed and knocked down my dresser. I screamed for them to get out. They went outside, but continued to bang on the door until it broke. I knew the nurse heard the commotion but she ignored it. I got tired of controlling myself and grabbed a stick that I hid in the room for protection; it was heavy like a pipe and had nails in it. They banged, pushed the door open and charged me. In the lead was the big shot, Barbara. I really wanted to hurt her and beat her with the stick. I also held a razor blade and cut her up; later she had to have fifty-two stitches sewed across her face. The other girls were scared and ran away.

After that, I got respect. The girls would meet me in the dining room and say, "Vivian, do you want this or that". I always told them, "leave me alone" but it didn't matter, they would come and give me things. I would just take it to throw away because I didn't want anything from people who had hurt me.

They transferred me to another building where the girls were older There I met a girl named Susan, who tried the same shit but I learned my lesson. I fought with her a lot though I don't like to fight; that is not me. Basically I am a friendly person but I was going to let them hurt me. I learned we were all in the same boat; sometimes there is happiness but mostly there is hard times and suffering.

I was there for four years though it seemed like a life time. At sixteen, I was discharged and returned home. While I was packing my bags, I was frightened, not knowing what to expect next. When I arrived, my little brothers, the ones whom I love the most, were the only ones to welcome me. My mother met me with the words, "Vivian, you don't have to stay here; you can leave anytime". It was like she was pushing me out before I arrived. I felt so unwelcome that I decided to go. Everything I had brought, the toys for my bothers, the clothes for my sister, I left for them.

Back on the Streets

I was back on the streets again but this time I didn't even know where the hell I was. In a daze, I took the subway to Manhattan. I had never been there before and I just got off on any stop. The stop was here in East Harlem.

It was just like when I was twelve, but only four years later and nothing mattered; I let everybody have sex with me. One morning I met this dude; he seemed to be a bad man. He was a heavy drinker but I said to myself, "what the hell, I haven't got anything to loose; one more won't hurt". Funny thing, he eventually saved me. He had a bottle and I heard his drinking friend tell him, "why don't you take that girl…everybody is taking advantage and using her. Take her under your wings".

I had sex with him that night and then after, he beat the hell out of me. The next morning we went out together and we met another of his friends who seemed to have money. I thought to myself, "I am starving, I need to get something to eat". I had been out there on the streets for several days with hardly any food. Sure I had nickels, dimes and quarters but hardly enough to buy a container of milk. My mind then was like mush and everything seemed invisible to me.

So I went with the guy with money to a hotel yet I didn't have sex with him. I was naked but I was in a daze. It was as if I was paralyzed. Someone might have thought I was stupid or dumb but that was not the case. I was just repeating to myself, over and over; "they are all the same. I might as well live this way, ruining my life because nobody cares".

The next morning we returned to the same corner and again met the guy who had previously beat me. I learned his name was Pablo. His friend threw me at him, "here Pablo, take this bitch". I shuddered, hearing "bitch" which was everybody's nasty description of me. He yelled, "she doesn't know how to do nothing". I thought, "it's not that I didn't know how, I just didn't want to. I felt dead".

I was crying as they talked about me as if I didn't exist but to my surprise Pablo took me back. I didn't understand why, thinking perhaps he was sorry for me. Maybe he took pity because I was so young, but in fact, I felt old and broken.

Love and Violence

We moved in together, to a tiny, filthy apartment in the Bronx. Pablo was drinking everyday, hallucinated and I thought to myself, "this man is crazy and I am now trapped with a nut". But yet in that little place, I felt safe and despite the drinking, he taught me how to cook. He would sing a beautiful song that he created for a girlfriend he once loved. When he told me about her, I felt hurt and asked, "what in the hell are you doing with me?" He told me that he felt sorry for me. When I heard that, I thought, "it's about time somebody did…somebody cared enough".

Often his friends would visit our place and I noticed when he spoke about me, he would call me his "woman". I couldn't stand that phrase because it made me feel that somehow he possessed me.

One time, a Spanish friend of his was visiting and Pablo went out to get a bottle of wine. The guy tried to kiss me. I refused, telling him, "I love Pablo", though of course I wouldn't admit that to him. I screamed at him, "you are nothing but trash, why would I want you to touch me!" The word "trash" triggers something in me; people used to call me "trash" but what the hell, nobody can hurt me anymore. I had been hurt so much, I couldn't feel no more pain. I just felt helpless.

The guy tried to kiss me in the ear. I pushed him away and ran to the door. He tried to grab me but stopped when he heard Pablo's footsteps on the stairway. Pablo met him on the stairs and asked "where are you going, man? ("man" and "bitch" were his favorite words). The guy played innocent but Pablo saw me nervous, shaking and crying and demanded to know what happened. I told him how the guy tried to get me and it slipped from my mouth, "I love you Pablo and I didn't want him to touch me". He asked me to repeat what I said. I thought I might as well say it and let it out again because it was true; he was the first man I really loved. Unlike the other men who used me, he did good things for me. Whenever he sang that song directed to that other woman, I would cry in my heart because I wanted it to be about me.

At night, lying in bed we listened to our tiny radio and sang together; nobody was bothering me and for that moment, I felt safe. At other times, he would hallucinate from the drinking. He must have believed he was Hercules or something and would get up and turn the bed upside down. I used to say, "Pablo, what in the hell are you doing?" He would then calm down and even apologize.

Later, we moved into a hotel in East Harlem and again I had trouble with his friends. One night, Pablo was out very late and scared, I kept peeking outside, hoping he would return. I bumped into one of his friends who invited me into his room to talk. The crazy thing was he took off his clothes while we talked. He tried to hold me but I refused to go near him. I swear by God, by my own son, he never touched me. Finally I discouraged him and he let me go, saying "I don't want to cause trouble". Meanwhile Pablo arrived and I explained I had been talking with his friend, Johnny. He went to check on Johnny and found him naked. Pablo then accused me of having sex with him. At first Johnny denied it but the next day when I wasn't around, he told Pablo that he had me. Later when I heard this from Pablo, I explained that the guy was a liar, telling one story in the night and another during day. I hated that guy for what he did to both us. I felt he was toying with me, trying to trick me and I fell for it.

Several nights later, there were some guys smoking pot and drinking in the hallway. They were talking real loud about raping and gang banging me. I begged Pablo, "please, let's leave tomorrow morning". He tried to reassure me, but I told him, "its okay for you to talk but I'm the one who will be getting raped, not you". The next morning as were leaving, those guys were out there and wanted to know when we were coming back. Pablo told them, "tonight" but thank god we never showed up again.

We moved back to a hotel in East Harlem and it was there that I found out I was having Pablo's child. This was important for both us, because Pablo was always talking about how never had the chance to take care of his kids and he wanted another son. I wasn't really trying to get pregnant but in a way, I wanted it to happen. When he came home, I told him, "I'm with your child". He seemed happy for a couple of days until he met his old friends. When he told them about the child, they said nasty things, "by that bitch that fucks everybody in the neighborhood". That blew him up.

The next day, Pablo brought another woman to our bedroom. I was furious, screaming, "why are you doing that" When she left, I told him I was finished with him and he gotta get out. He tried to apologize, explaining that he believed I had sex with his friend and he was paying me back. I thought to myself, to take revenge that way, right in front of me, such a person has to have a lot of craziness inside of him.

The following night, we met that same girl who said, "Vivian, your husband fucked me last night; well I am going to have his baby". That got us both mad. I felt she was a no good tramp, that everybody in the hotel had her. Later I went to her room, while Pablo waited outside of the door. I barged into the room and yelled, "are you really going to have my old man's baby?" When she said "yea", I asked her to tell it again to his face. I told her, "wait a minute, I left something in the hallway"; that something was Pablo. I called for Pablo but though she begged me not to continue, I replied, "why not, are you guilty or something?" When Pablo entered, she put up this front and said "yea, I am gonna have your baby". Pablo then slapped her hard in the face and I know if he was angry that he was capable of killing her. I held him back, telling him, she wasn't worth it. But then I got started, beating her to a point where I couldn't stop though part of me knew that it was a bad thing to do. I broke her nose and busted her lip open. While we fought, I even turned her bed upside down on top of her. I really felt like hurting that girl. Pablo helped, holding her hair while I punch. Finally he ordered me to stop but I couldn't and he had to just drag me off of her. As we leaving, I hit her on the side of the head with my shoe and dropped a heavy fan on her toes. Later Pablo told me he liked to see women fight over him; he really enjoyed it.

By the next day, everybody in the hotel heard of the fight. The hotel was filled with psychiatric patients and the way I saw it, it was a hotel of nuts, made helpless by their medication. One man suggested that I calm down by taking medication, but I believe if I took that stuff it would just me crazy.

We continued to have trouble at the hotel. I noticed my mood changed and I didn't know what to do with myself. I felt so strange that I started tearing apart the hotel, even breaking down a door. I felt that in some way Pablo was haunting me.

I was constantly jealous and I had good reason. One of the maids told me, "Pablo should be my man, not yours. I yelled back, "maid or no maid, get out of my doorway…Pablo is too good for you. You will have to lick the ground before you have him". After that incident she gave me clothes but I believe she just wanted to get close to me so that she could catch Pablo. Before we left that hotel, I shoved the clothes into her face.

I had a run in with another woman there. Sometimes I babysat for her kid and I would listen to her brag about how she never fought with her husband. She was in fantasy land; having had seven children and gave almost all of them up. I borrowed a book from her and one night after baby sitting, she demanded the book. When I refused, she shouted and pushed me. I ran to my room, returned with the book and ripped it up in front of her, yelling, "you can eat the pages for all I care".

We were not liked there and finally we were thrown out and ended back on the streets. We slept in hallway, rooftops and the park. I was so cold that Pablo would give me his jacket and even shirt, to keep me from freezing. As for him, he always had a bottle to keep him warm. To his credit, when he hustled money, before he spent it on wine, he would make sure we had enough to be eat and that I was properly nourished.

The homeless life finally ended, when my angel at the hospital, a social worker, managed to get me into a maternity home. I remained there until she helped get things straight with welfare.

After all the hurt and pain, I had Pablo's son; it was worth it. He is a beautiful little boy. When Pablo first saw the baby, he was shocked. Part of him didn't believe it could be his child. It slowly dawned on him that this was his son. I told him, "Pablo, when I love, I love for real. I don't play with love and I don't play with life…Remember, I've always stuck by you, honored you and will do so, even after your death". Pablo responded by teasing me, that he felt I couldn't live without him. Now I can give as much as I can take, "Hmmmh, what makes you think so? I've had enough men to last a lifetime." He laughed when he heard that.

During our time together, I have tried to convince him to stop drinking, telling him to do it, "not for me, not for your son but for yourself. That wine is going to kill you. No matter how many times I've told you to drop dead, I love you too much to see that happen". He tried; got detoxed in the hospital, came out, drank again and went in again. The last time, he remained for a long time and when he was discharged, he was fine. Still, as always, he carried that look of the devil on his face. With him, one has to take it or leave it; never knowing what to expect.

After the delivery, my mother invited me with my son, back home. It was my intention to get along and not argue or fight. Pablo was in agreement since otherwise we would be homeless. I stayed there as best I could. I cleaned, kept quiet but when my son cried at night, my mother acted as if it was a crime. Soon, she got real loud and critical with me and even with Pablo. When he visited, she told him, "you are the father, why don't you buy things for your son". Pablo would get real upset and one night when he arrived late, he was pushed too far.. My mother yelled, "what in the hell is he doing up here so late?" I started to cry, trying to explain, but it didn't do no good. My mother, joined by her husband got on my case and she screamed, "Vivian get the hell out of this house before I throw you and that baby down the stairs". Pablo was real furious and told them "no you ain't; unless we're all going die in this house, right now". I knew he was capable of killing them. It was time to leave right then.

We loaded ourselves up, carrying the baby and his things. We got on the train and traveled in the middle of the night, all the way from Brooklyn to East Harlem. It was raining and cold and we all huddled together in an abandoned building. Luckily, Pablo's friend was around and warned him, "watch out before that kid catches pneumonia…I don't give a fuck about you two. You can make it on the street but he can't". He invited us into his place.

The next morning, I sought out my guardian angel, the social worker. She had done more for me than my own mother and I made her my son's god mother.

As always, she came through and found a temporary place for the baby. Eventually I got on welfare and received money. But in the mean time, it was pure hell. I was out there, hungry, so tired and getting weaker by the day. I was starving. With my first check, I ate like there was no tomorrow.

Now I am happy. I got on welfare and an apartment that I can call my own. I have a son that I can call my own. I have a man that I love and he loves me. My

Pablo is even working and straightening out. This is what I've been looking for all my life and I'm never going to let go of this. The past is all behind me.

Reflection

You know, I'm looking back and thinking of those niggers in my life who I miss and cared for. I hear a voice telling me, "always try to love people".

It was my grandfather, who used to swing and pick me up. This grandfather told me to write but I was too young to figure out the address. I can no longer remember his face. I no longer know what anybody looks like outside my family. I don't know what my aunts, uncles or cousins look like. But I always remember what he told me, even though I was real little and it was a long time ago; "don't walk away like you don't love me because I love you".

Postscript

After several months, Pablo went on a drinking binge which took the form of alcoholic psychosis; he was hospitalized in a psychiatric wing. After his discharge, he returned to his old neighborhood and had a number of altercations. There he was accused of sexually molesting a twelve year old child. Though he denied the accusation, he was arrested and is out on bail.

Vivian's new life almost came to a tragic end. On the street, Vivian was accosted by a man; when she rejected his overtures, he shot her three times.

Pablo and Vivian are survivors; for the time being, they are living together in an apartment with their son.

4

Profile of a Teenage Prostitute

Alice is one of those street wise but angry youngsters, who might have stepped out of central casting for the classic, Taxi Driver. Her life history contradicts much of the romantic myths and fantasies of the "working girl".

The Setting

Close to the carbon monoxide entrance to the midtown tunnel on 34th St., Alice works out of a shabby and drab basement apartment. Because of the lack of ventilation, a visitor might feel chocked and suffocated. Despite these conditions the rent is high and the landlord probably receives "extra" because of the illegal activity. Alice partners up with Sharon who had worked in public relations firm but after it closed down decided "to do for money what she used to do for free with the big shot clients".

Both work together as a team and as Alice explains, "like I'm 17 and she is 22, so I am younger but she is more educated. She is tall and skinny and I am medium size and nicely built. They got their pick".

They were not alone in the apartment. Also present were two simply dressed women and a heavily built, sullen looking, middle aged man. Alice stands out; not only because of sex appeal, amplified by a tight sweater and pants but due to her vivaciousness. She drew me aside and explained the situation.

"This guy sitting over there is our slave"; she pointed across the room. Like if one of us has to go to the bathroom, we can order him to accompany us and clean up after. He is paying us $200 for allowing us to be his master. He addresses me as "mistress" and only acknowledges female dominance. He hates men and refuses to submit to them. It is only to us women that he is a slave." She points over to two girls sitting in the corner, noting, they are just "squares". They live next door and visit to pass the time and watch this crazy scene.

My Family

I wonder sometimes how I ended up here? I could start with my father. He was brutal, especially to me. Whenever I got a chance I would disappear from home to escape his drunken anger. He was an alcoholic like most of his family. My mother managed to stay with him and during their twenty-seven years together, they had eleven kids. I am second to the oldest. My eldest sister is nineteen and is married. There were three other children who died prior to my birth. On top of this, I have a mentally retarded brother. The family went through a lot of changes, from welfare to one what would call, lower, middle class. Over the years, my father couldn't handle the changes and stress and it just made him more belligerent and alcoholic. Still he managed to work in the mills and support us.

Near my seventeenth birthday, the old man told me "to get out of the house". Like we had this big fight and he pulled a butcher knife on me. That wasn't something new. Before he would hit and punch me into unconsciousness. This time he chased me around the yard with a knife. It was a close call.

Usually when we fought, the police would intervene and he would end up in jail. They usually let him out after he sobered up. He would try AA, attend for a while but then fall into one of his dark moods. I believe the reason he would get drunk was that he couldn't say what was inside him. You know, some people are unable to look at you and say "I am angry" or "I love you"; my father is one of these people. Only when drunk did he say what was going on inside of him but it was so crazy. I both hate and love him.

My mom was a true survivor. All the shit he put her through; it is a miracle she isn't in the nut house by now. She had three nervous breakdowns but yet, was able to raise us. In some ways, we had a "straight" family. We always lived in the same house and had parents. My mother would attend church every Sunday. Both of them are religious. In their own way, they are close and don't cheat on each other. I don't even believe they even think about that stuff.

All in all, except for my father's drinking, my family might seem normal.

Still it was the times he was violently drunk, that affected and damaged something inside of me. At fifteen, I was so wild, that he arranged to put me in a detention home. By this time I had run away, six times. If I felt a beating was coming, I would leave for a few days or even a week. I would stay with guys who had their own apartments and jobs, so I wouldn't have to worry about taking care of myself.

Neither parent trusted me in contrast to my older sister; their perfect child.

She was only two years older but at my age was allowed to go out on her own. I was labeled the "wild one". They believed if I was going to go out with my boyfriend, I was going to fuck. They didn't think my sister was into it but she was doing exactly the same thing. I was always guilty. My sister was momma's little girl and I was the "black sheep". The truth was my sister was being "banged" way before me but I was seen as the "whore" of the family. It wasn't that way. I waited until I was sixteen but I let everyone believe that I was bad.

I always felt different and never could stand anybody telling me what to do. Asking me is "okay" but as for telling me; "you might as well hang it up". I guess I was more adventuresome and "pigheaded" then most girls. I would be the first one to start smoking. I would be the first one to steal from a store. I was ten when I first became aware that I marched to a different tune. I attended a Catholic school which charged a high tuition but my grandfather paid for it. There were only two blacks there; a brother and sister. I was the first one in the entire school to accept and hang out with them. I was the only one to go out with a black guy. I continued even when the white girls tried to pressure me. Eventually I got kicked out of that school. First I received 4 suspensions because of skipping classes, smoking and stuff like that. Finally they just didn't want me there no more.

In a way I am like my old father. When he was sixteen, he got into trouble and quit school. Maybe we are too much alike. I did things to aggravate him. He couldn't deal with me. Like the school, he said, "just leave, I can't handle you anymore". When I heard that, I said to myself, "fuck everybody I am going to live my own life the way I want to".

I believe my parents know what I do. It doesn't take much to figure out, given that I shift back and forth from Pittsburgh and New York. At first my mother believed I found an office job but after conversations with me, she was able to piece it all together. I didn't have to declare, "hey, I have been lying", because she knew it and had to accept it." Her view is once you leave home, "you make your own bed". She doesn't like the way I live and is hurt by it but what can she do; nothing. She knows she can't come stomping over to New York and demand I return. She just accepts my fate. As for my father, if he ever overcomes his denial, he would probably kill me in a drunken rage.

Learning the Ropes

Here is how I learned the ropes. When I left home, just jail bait, I stayed with this steel worker guy. He was Black, tough but an okay dude. He then passed me onto his friend who wined and dined me but at very cheap places. He tells me, "so and so ain't going to support you". I explained that I just left home and I need to find my way. I add that I am not thinking of getting a job right now. He asked, did I know what I wanted to do and what did I do best? I gave him the perfect answer for him; "I fuck but anybody can do that" After our conversation he introduces me to another guy who offer a round trip ticket to New York City and a guarantee that I could make two thousand dollars in seven days. He explains that I will be working for a madam, who will supply the customers.

I always jump feet first into new things and took the ticket and off to New York. Of course I was scared, even flying was a new thing for me. I didn't even know where Queens was located but I made it there. A black guy and woman ran the house located in a two bedroom apartment. I worked and slept there.

I was really busy, seeing several guys a day, working from the afternoon to midnight. Finished on Saturday, I returned to Pittsburgh. There, I gave the money to the guy who I was temporarily staying with. The pimp who set up the connection didn't receive anything but his interest was my education into the life. He just wanted me to have a training experience.

I was then invited to go to Bermuda. I thought to myself, this guy is really nuts, thinking that I was going to feed his greed by peddling my ass for him. I know I was dumb to give him the money in the first place but still he had a nice apartment and gave me money for clothes. Also I figured through his contact I would learn about the trade, make connections and, then go off to New York. In fact that was what I did, ditching him.

Here, I was helped by a guy who introduced me to the night scene. He was a pusher, not a pimp, but knew all about the "life". At first, I was suspicious, since when we first met he seemed too friendly. Also, I knew that I didn't want to be with a guy who collected money from my work. When I told him that "I turned tricks", he was cool, saying "oh you do", and that was it. Never once did he try to pull a number, like, "why don't you and me pool our money together". He was a coke pusher and there were problems because I was paranoid about being busted. Even worst I started sniffing the stuff. Things became really heavy when he started mixing the coke with heroin. I really got worried when he also started selling straight heroin. I felt that I was going to be hooked on the shit and maybe he was setting me up. I split, escaping from him and the dope.

I then worked for various madams. Actually, it was rare to find a man running a house. The routine in the houses were pretty much the same. The madam would maintain a private telephone book and would reach out to the "Johns" and remind them of the girls or they would make inquiries. When the "John" arrives, he would be given a drink and then make his pick. We would be waiting in a sexy outfit; dressed like in doll pajamas or skimpy bikinis. If I was picked, we would go off into the bedroom and he would tell me what was sexual preference and I like an actress, would perform; usually it was fucking or a blow job. He would pay the madam a price and she was supposed to split it. Of course, I never new if she was charging more then she was claiming. On the other hand, I was supposed to split the tip but it was never more then ten dollars and I would keep it for myself. The fact is, for someone not even eighteen, making over $1,000 per week was pretty good. But of course it is great to be a madam; if you multiply by four girls, she is making four thousand a week, a great deal of money by any standards. Furthermore, having once been prostitutes, they really know the inside/out of the business.

My fantasy is that by the time I am thirty, to have my own operation. I plan to have four girls, not do anything and get half their earnings. It will take time because I plan to build up a clientele and then have a good client base.

I was no dummy and I learned how to beat the madam at her game. If the client was a good spender, I would make a deal on the side. I would give him my number and try to obtain his. Then on my own, I would call and invite him for a date. Of course, the madam would counter this strategy by promising the client a "freebee" if he got my number.

A Routine Life

I have no problem with what I do. I simply like making money the easy way. This sure beats the straight job I have had; McDonalds, dish washer and nurses aide. Furthermore, I don't like people telling me what to do; here I am my own person. I hate the idea that I have to live by the clock. This way, even if a John wants to meet and I am not in the mood, I just cancel. I can go out when I want; get up when I want; go where I want.

I am a lazy person and wake up about noon. About 1:00, I am open for business. I will call some of the Johns or just wait around. My partner in crime, Sharon, is good company and we just pass the day, as guys come and go. At midnight, my business shuts down. Usually, I return to my apartment, take a shower and stay up watching T.V. until about 4:00 am. Sometimes I will make to the after hour bars. The next day, the routine continues though at times I will sleep as much as fourteen hours; just as long as I want to.

Sunday is my day off (this is not completely accurate since our interview occurred then and she was reaching out via the phone to customers). I will chill out; call my family, write letters and hang out with a friend, Betty is an ex-prostitute but switched into selling cocaine. We visit the country with her car to just get away from it all. Other times we will get high, dine, go to movies or walk in Central Park. I am just like everybody else in this city except I cater to the needs of men.

One of my concerns is the handling of money. No matter how much I earn, I find it impossible to save. Money burns in my hands. Maybe deep down, I feel the "money is dirty" and I need to get rid of it. There are days when I make one thousand dollars and somehow I would end up with nothing to show for all my work. My spending habits include everything. I might begin by buying boxes of Godiva chocolate; I have a sweet tooth. Then there would be lotions and perfume. And as for spending on clothes, forget it. I only go to the classy boutiques which make me feel unique and different. Watching money disappear, I now ask my mother to be my banker. I trust her and this way whenever I am in need, I know the savings are there. This solution has allowed me to save thousands of dollars though I never keep count.

The John

I noticed men have certain patterns. I can predict when I will be busy. Mondays are good days, probably because the husbands are returning from a weekend of fights with their wives and need me for relief. Somehow, Wednesday is busy, maybe kind of a midweek break. Fridays are slow. I am busy when it rains; perhaps guys like to fuck when it rains or that they are "bummed out" and need a lift. One day it was pouring and in a few hours I made several hundred dollars. The weather was terrible and I couldn't believe that these guys kept calling and coming over; nonstop. It is like this thing with them; when it is most dark or depressing outside, they need to come to see me.

I believe fucking with me is different and easier for them. Why should they call a regular girl; wait for her to get dressed and never know what will happen. Instead with me, they know what to expect and they will be able to get off.

I noticed that because of lay offs, there is a lot of insecurity and the men are not spending so freely. This is especially true with the corporate guys. They probably think, "do I spend $150 on the hooker or keep the money for a rainy day?"

The phone rings and she responds with a double message. Verbally she is coquettish to the John, but her facial expressions display contempt as she exclaims, "Bob, you creep, why haven't you been calling? Didn't I please you?" In a quiet, seductive voice, "I miss you". Apparently the John explains that he has a date and she asks him to forgo it for a session with her. After he hangs up, Barbara is angry at her failure. "He is a real creep. This guy usually spends just $75 for one half hour and yet I know he has lots of money. He hasn't called in a long while and it seems to me like he is getting off just hearing my voice. This guy is a real dud; something is wrong with him. My view is everybody is off, particularly men; they are sick and perverted. There are a lot of "sickies". Guys come here and ask me to beat them or to dress up in my clothes. I wonder to myself how do these people get started and become like that?"

Rip off

Several months later, she was depressed and overwhelmed. She explained that everything was going fine but because of her mother's illness, she returned home to take care of her younger siblings. While away, I let this chic stay at my house and gave her permission to service whoever wanted to see me. In exchange, she would be responsible for the rent. I was stupid because she stole the customers and never even paid for the telephone bill. I lost my clients.

Desperate, I went into the street. It can be really rough there. I checked out Eighth Ave. and 48th St. Waiting on the corner I noticed this black guy strutting toward me. He wore blue jeans, muscle type sweater and spoke with a Spanish accent. Conning me, he asks for my girlfriend. I explain that I work alone. Then he gives me the rap that he swore I was the girl from last night. He asks me to go out for seventy five dollars and because I was desperate, I accepted.

We entered the hotel room and his voice becomes harsh, "hey babe, when you first started doing this, didn't anybody tell you not to out with Black dudes whom you don't know". He turned this ring around on his finger and it has this sharp diamond. Holding it toward my face, he demanded all my money.

Like that wasn't enough. He then tied me to the bed and fucked me in the ass and everything. After finishing with me, he asked, "do you have an old man?" He told me "you can't work in this city if you don't have an old man". I pretended to go along with whatever he wanted. He invited me downstairs to meet his "woman" and assumed that I was now his "bitch". I met her but more important I memorized the license of his car.

Though I was really shook up, I looked up the number of a gangster acquaintance. He once told me if I was in any trouble, to get in touch. His gig was kidnapping pushers, holding them for ransom and shit like that.

We found his address through the license plate and my friend took over. He handcuffed him to a pipe in a basement for three days and scared the crap out of him. He was told that unless he came up with twenty-five grand, it was the end. The guy finally called his old lady and the money was ours. We split it.

While waiting for the money I enjoyed watching the pimp sweat. I wanted him to suffer and to teach him respect so that he wouldn't ever again try that on me. I learned a tough lesson; be careful because you never know who you are messing with in this business.

The Law

You can see why I hate the street but there is another reason; the law. I got busted thirty times for soliciting and I was before this one judge, four times in a row. I hired a lawyer, who received five hundred for each appearance. At the last time, the judge declared, "Riker's Island, 15 to 30 days". He banged his hammer and my lawyer can only tell me "well, he is the judge". I yelled, "you dirty son of a bitch, you got my money, but what good did it do!" I was returned to the holding cell and had to bribe the matron to again get the lawyer. The lawyer told me that he can get me out if I raise one thousand dollars for the judge. I was furious but relieved, thinking, "this is cool because I don't have to do time". I contacted a friend who passed the money onto the lawyer. Do you know what? The judge dismissed the whole case.

The cops are no better or even worse. They would hassle me, demanding free blow jobs. I always refused I would tell them, "only if you give me five dollars is it a deal." It was the principle; I would rather go to jail then do it for free. I saw those guys as blackmailers. Either they wanted a blow job, money or else they pull you in. It is not only the pimps but even the law pimps off the prostitutes.

The whole city is full of shit and the prostitutes are unfairly picked on. I know they are trying to get rid of us because of the tourist trade and the city image. In fact, it is the girls who are pick pockets that hurt the image; it is the women who play the "Murphy" bit, or make believe they are going to sleep with the guy and then have a phony boyfriend break into the room and demand money. We do a service not only for the guys but their wives. If those guys didn't have us, they would be frustrated and cheat on their wives. In a way we are needed in this city.

Image

I can easily tell those who are in the "life" and the "squares". It is just something about us and them. Certainly, our life style is different. We hang out in after-hour bars until six am. There we snort or smoke pot. The rooms are filled with black guys, black women and white girls. Squares are discouraged from entering. To be considered part of this life, you either are a pusher, con man, pimp or prostitute. If I attempt to bring in a straight dude, management would immediately pick it up and stop us. They could tell just by looking at us. There is a certain way that people carry themselves that reveal who they are. I immediately notice if a woman is a prostitute or a man, a pimp. It is the way they talk and conduct themselves. There also the many unwritten rules of this "life" that the squares cannot even begin to understand. You just absorb it as if you picked up a new accent. It just wears on you, even without realizing it.

When I first entered the "life", a lot of guys would respond; "you're so young, so cute; you must be a student". I approached a lot of guys but they refused, not believing that I was a "working girl". Actually, I thought that was fantastic. I never wanted anybody to label me as a common "prostitute". Many people think of prostitutes as street walkers, strutting about with their short skirts and tight sweaters. I hate the idea that in public I might be seen or labeled me as a prostitute. I admit though, a subtle change has happened. It has gotten to a point when I simply take a walk guys respond as I am a hooker.. I ask myself what are the signals, to make them think this way? Once after being approached, I asked the guy, "what am I doing to make you think this way?" He told me, "I can tell just by the way you look around when you're walking and how you talk". It seems I am carrying myself as a hooker without even realizing it. The idea that people can tell really gets to me. I never wanted to project myself this way. Even when I have a client, I try to be subtle and not crude. Because I am so friendly and relaxing, there are times guys will attempt to walk out without leaving anything, completely forgetting that our arrangement is about money. If he is a regular customer, I keep quiet, knowing that I can remind him the next time. My style is never to demand the money up front, because it turns both of us off. Maybe it is the Polish pride of my ancestors but I would rather the "Johns" think of me as a person, a lady, before anything else.

Wishful Thinking

Although I would never return home, I often think of "what if": if I stayed, had a nice boyfriend, attended school, live with my family and did what everyone else does? Yet I cannot go back to the old life. I would never be satisfied with the world at home or a simple job. I could never return, knowing that I make so much money for practically doing nothing.

Still there is a part of me that wishes to get married, have two kids, live in Florida and have a suburban house, like everybody else. But right now there are so many things to do and so many places to go. This is one of the fastest ways to earn money without hurting anybody and I am good at it. I even think that with all the money that I stash away, I could be married and not have to be dependent on any husband. I will always be my own person. As to the question of telling him the source, it would depend on the person and the situation. This is just speculation because needing someone is not one of my hang-ups. Right now, I have no intention of settling down. I look forward to traveling and enjoying life.

An Overview of the Life

We have no close friends; we just have acquaintances. We can't trust anybody in this business. It is cut-throat competition with everybody trying to stab the other in the back. Jealousy, lying, larceny and greed; they are all part of our way. Our obsession is to get ahead by any means. We never look back or to the future. It is how we score today that counts. The feeling is that we can always peddle our asses, steal, pick pockets, con or sell drugs, etc. We are not like the squares that worry about being lay offs or not selling a product or going bankrupt. We are free. We figure all the money we made is due us though deep down, we all know, "we got to pay a price, to play this game".

5

"God Keeps Kicking Me in the Ass"

Though I knew her as Wanda, I was told by the social worker that introduced us, she was known on the streets as "Wanda White Cloud". At the time of our first meeting, she was seven month's pregnant, tired and exhausted. Though just thirty-one, she had the haggard look of a middle aged, street lady. She seemed depressed but masked it with a false bravado. My first impression was that of a lost and broken soul, but she was possessed with a frightening, powerful rage that could be lethal.

Not only was the frailty of her appearance deceptive, but also her manner of speech. She was of German-American ancestry yet her accent was Hispanic. She slipped into ghetto jargon when she was excited.

Although she never completed fifth grade and academically uneducated, her intellectual abilities should not be underestimated, having mastered Spanish, Polish and German. Her social worker informed me that she thought Wanda was mildly retarded. What seemed to authorities as limited intelligence was in fact Wanda's way of manipulating by pretending helplessness. She kept hidden her strengths and destructiveness and was possessed with a ruthlessness that led to murder.

"I Was the One They Kicked Around"

I was born with my twin sister in an auto part's store in the Bronx. There was a snow storm and my mother couldn't make it to the hospital. They put us both in shoe boxes; a great way of entering this world.

There were twelve of us; eight boys and four girls. My mother was an angel and my father never had much to do with us kids. When he returned from work, I was expected to be absolutely silent and cringed in his presence. If I even coughed or made a noise, he would yell, "what the fuck is wrong with you" and smack me across the head. My brothers and sisters sometimes got it but I felt that I was the one chosen to receive the dirty end of the deal. I quickly learned he was the man with the iron fist.

For example, when I was twelve and my eldest sister ran away to New Jersey, mother asked me to bring her clean clothes. The old man found out, took out his brass knuckles and beat me to a pulp. Yea, he sure loved to use his hands and if not the brass knuckles then it was the garrison belt. I would be thrown about like corner like a piece of junk. What made it worse was that nobody would defend me or even have anything to do with me.

I lived in total fear. I never knew when or what part of my body or face would be bashed. It was always "hush, hush" with me. I was the type of kid who would quietly sit and assume that eventually I would be blamed and beaten.

Rage grew inside, ready to explode. It first came out when I was about seven but it is hard for me to remember the details, no less talk about it. My mother was hanging clothes on the roof while my twin and I waited nearby. A demon seemed to posses me. I turned on her, smashing in her skull. It is not clear how it happened and to this day I can't believe I did it. I keep telling myself she fell but I know that I tried to kill her. The old man got revenge on me. There were beatings and beatings until my poor little body couldn't take it anymore. My legs were so badly damaged that I was unable walk for three months. Even today, you can feel the creases in my scalp where he used the brass knuckles.

I remember escaping with my mother and kid sister in her arms from one of his rages to the police station. The old man didn't care, always yelling, "sure tell them, tell them what I do". Usually she kept quiet fearing that he would get her later. I guess she remained with him for many reasons. He had a good job as an engineer and we needed his money. She was also tied to him because in a strange way she loved him. To me it was sick but then I could never understand the relationship between man and woman. Most of my early life, I wished he would die or dreamed that I would kill him. When I was as young as seven, while he was beating my mother, I thought of stabbing him in the back with a kitchen knife. Hell, how pitiful to have these thoughts, at such a young age!

I lived in total fear. I never knew when it would either be me or my mother. It didn't matter how severe, whether my face or body would get bashed, the message was "shut up". No wonder I was a bundle of nerves. It didn't help that I was a weak child, often suffering from pneumonia. I recall that even when the other kids got coats, I wasn't given one. Without proper clothing, I was freezing in winter. A large part of childhood was spent at St. Vincent's Hospital. Despite that, I don't blame my mom. She tried to protect me but wasn't strong enough.

To me she was my angel, pampering me when I was ill, slipping me extra food and bandaging the cuts.

My life has been hell. When I was eleven, my father found a way to kick me out of the family. Alice, a friend, stole trip that was kept in the kindergarten room. Because I was known to the grocery store owner, she asked me to buy cigarettes there. At first I didn't realize the money was stolen. I thought I was doing her a favor. The authorities were determined to find out the thieves and one day they left money with invisible dye. Unfortunately Alice again stole, this time with me as the accomplice. It was about two o'clock when the principal entered the room; my mother was standing outside the door. He demanded that I show my show hands. They must have suspected us from the beginning.

Because of the old man's insistence, at eleven years old they sent me away and I didn't return until a few years later. In thinking back, I realize I was hard to handle and a troublemaker but there was no reason to kick me out. What really hurt, was the feeling my mother deserted me. As for him, I continued to have fantasies of killing him, though I escaped several times, never attempted it.

Later, when I came of age, "the shoe was on the other foot". My mother moved to Florida and whenever there was extra money, I helped her out. As for that "fucker", when I was older and got out in the world, I confronted him. I told him not to mess with me, that I had my nigger friends to back me and if need be, he would be killed. Since then, whenever we would meet he would cringe and in a begging way, say for example, "Wanda, your mother would like to know if she could borrow a hundred dollars". I would remind him that my mother could have the money but "none of it was for him".

You see, I don't think of my parents as two, but only as one; my mother. I know she is broken hearted about my life. She is aware of the drugs but never shows it. When I visit, I bring a few gifts and carry my Jewish bankroll, along with bottles of "meth" (methadone) to tide me over. Despite calling it "blood money" she accepts the dough. She stashes it away for me, though last Christmas she asked my permission to buy a trailer. My kid sister was deserted by her "old man" and at first asked to join me. I knew that would destroy her so I told my mother it was okay to use the money to help her. As for the others, we have nothing to say to each other and I believe they have turned against me. I don't like their square life and they can't figure out mine.

Now I am seven month's pregnant and want a child. I have had four miscarriages. I am thirty-one and I have been on the street for twelve years. Off and on, I have had a habit though this time I am determined to change my life. Maybe because of the drugs I have failed but I believe this pregnancy will work out. On the other hand, I have doubts because God seems to keep kicking me in the ass.

Loving and Hating

At the New York Training School for Girls, I learned a lot about life. In the cottage, because I was the youngest and only white girl, I received a lot of attention. Mr. O., the housefather really adored me. In contrast, his wife was jealous and cold. Life there was amongst girls and we would play family. The elder Black girls would fight to have me as their "daughter". Since I was so young and tiny, I always played the child. When I got older, the family changed; no longer a child, I played the part of the mother choosing a husband, which would be another older girl. Later this all changed; I became the "fem" and tied myself to one of the hardest daddy's on campus, Snooky. We only "swapped spit", which is kissing and never went all the way. Only later did I learn what it meant to "go down" on a woman.

It was with Cherl that I realized a woman could stir another woman. I was just sixteen but I found myself throbbing when she passed by me. Finally with small feminine ways, a little eye contact, I got her attention. We became really close and I would still be with her but later she ended up doing "life" for murder. Sex with her was really fulfilling unlike with guys. It wasn't vulgar like people think. Our bodies connected as if we were man and woman but in this case it was woman and woman. The only difference there was no prick to insert. My mind wasn't stuck on the notion she was a woman but being fulfilled and excited. It was easy for her since she had always been comfortable as gay and acted like a male. Having spent so much time with girls in reform school, it was easy for me to make it with women. In contrast, perhaps being scared shit of my father, I was hung up about having a male and didn't begin until I was nineteen. Deep down, men always frightened me.

Overall, life in that reformatory wasn't too bad. There were fights because some of the girls were jealous of the attention given to me by the housefather. I believed he might have even loved me, not in a disrespectful manner, because he talked to me like the father that I never really had. Also I had a close girlfriend and my mother continued to write. Eventually they decided I was "together" enough to be transferred to a foster home.

There I stepped backwards into the "shit". They stuck me with a seventy year lady along with her pet; a big, fat girl, Dotty, who also was once in Cottage B. I was told to call her "sister" but I felt it was another one of those familiar, Cinderella scenes like in my family. First I was given the crap room while she had a large, lovely place, with white carpeting, a lace bedspread and the whole bit. Needless to say, I hated her.

I was enrolled in the same school as Dotty and she would try to introduce me as her little sister. I'd tell her, "don't you tell no mother-fucking lies, I 'm no sister of yours". Right out, I would admit, "I'm one of those from the training school and I am only here on a trial". I intended to play the authority's game because they wouldn't let me out until they believed I was fit for society. Deep down I felt that so-called society had been dumping garbage on me and when released, I intended to throw it right back. Because of my impatience it didn't work like I expected. I hated the old lady and I would go out at night or just run away. Even when she tried to lock me in, I would find a way out and if need be, jump from a high window. They finally gave up and sent me back to the reform school.

"Heroin Has Always Been My Love"

When I came of age, I was released and hung out with Latinos. These friends introduced me to after hour clubs and night spots and there I made new Black friends. I began to dig that life and those people dug me. I was naïve then and used by the pushers to hold their brown bags or silver foil wrappings. Sometimes the cops made a search and I'd be carrying the "shit". When I realized I was being suckered and taking risks, I demanded my due; it was then that I got into heavy dope. I have been on it since I was nineteen and now I am thirty-one.

Sure it is an expensive habit but lately I have reduced my daily need to eight spoons of heroin and one or two spoons of coke. Depending on the source, the cost averages from two hundred to two hundred twenty five dollars. Right now there is a war of turf between the pushers over who is going to take over the Turkish dope distribution. There is less of the Columbian or Brown Asian and more of the Turkish white stuff. The cost could be sixty dollars a quarter, thirty five for one half quarter which is less then a table spoon. It is rare today to find two or five dollar bags and instead there are mostly ten dollar bags. I would need six or seven ten dollar bags to keep myself just for the afternoon, waiting for the evening hustle which was either boosting or selling myself.

My craving has been for all types of dope. I enjoy coke but not as much as heroin. Those who snort are fools; it's a waste of money. With coke, my heart thumps real heavy. I sweat and smell an odor, like that in an antiseptic hospital. Initially it is a challenge, trying to keep calm but then I speed up with a desire to run and move. I find myself incessantly talking and sometimes get paranoid, wherein I might grab a bat for protection. In contrast, heroin is a different ball-game. I experience a nice mellow, drowsy feeling. My ideal is a combination called, "speedball". First, I heat the heroin then add one half spoon of coke. I get the best of both worlds; go up with the coke and heroin nicely brings me down. It is also economical because when I have coke there is an urge to run out and spend money. But with speedball, the heroin quiets and relaxes me. Of course if I had to make a choice, heroin is always my first love.

Street Survivor

My appearance is deceptive and to look at me, you wouldn't think I was tough and smart. I never completed the sixth grade but I consider myself an educated person. I have always been curious and while in prison, read extensively. I even wrote a paper, called "An Indictment Against Love". I try to keep my mind busy and have a working knowledge of three languages; German, Polish and Spanish. How many investment bankers can claim that?

Another type of knowledge that is more important is "street smarts". You need to be quick to survive out there. You can't be a "dummy" to support an expensive habit. For example, I worked as a cleaning lady in Yorkville (Upper East Side). To get that type of job, I learned to both blend and work hard. I cleaned houses and scrubbed floors on my bare knees. Most domestics don't go to that length but I had another agenda. I would check out the apartment and find where the valuables were hidden. I would win the lady's confidence and learn about her secret hide outs.

I have certain standards though and if I was treated decently, I cleaned their shit, washed their floors and didn't rip them off. When I felt "they fucked me, I fucked them back." I would rob them blind; to get revenge and also pick up extra dough, I would give blow jobs to their husbands. Admittedly, if my habit got too expensive, then all the rules were broken.

It has always been easy for me to both learn and survive on the streets. My best teachers were the "cons" in reform school. Even when I first got hooked, everything was cool. I was living with a group of pushers and they supplied me. Still I wanted my freedom. I eased away from them and looked for others ways to feed the habit.

I learned from a friend to take hustling, seriously, as a job. At 8:00 in the evening she would regularly and consistently go out and return by 11:30. She would score a few hundred in those few hours. After she rested, would then return to the streets from 1:00 am to 3:00 am. She probably could have made a great deal of money but she was young and not sophisticated or hip to her value. Still she earned enough to supply herself until the next day and have money left over. Initially, I wasn't so hip either, but I learned quickly. I asked her where was the best place to earn a few hundred bills without having to rob. She steered me to 86th street and gave me advice how to keep cool out there. I was told to find the going price and gain an idea of the territory.

The usual message is, "you do your thing but don't get in the way of our thing". If you break the rules sometimes there are consequences. One of the uptown bitches got stabbed three times in the head because she charged twenty dollar to a "trick" who usually spends seventy-five. You need to learn quickly or you are gonna be dead. By some standards, I was a success. I was the first one amongst the girls to buy a Cadillac. At that time, I organized several girls and had them work for me on the streets. I put a roof over their heads, gave them clean clothes and in a way provided a home. To my way of thinking, I benefited myself but also helped improve their lives. I was better then the pimps who beat them. Instead these girls looked to me for protection and help.

Even the law favored me. Once I was busted for "white slavery" but when the judge saw that I was a young woman and not a Black pimp, he responded "get this case out of here; you're kidding me that this young girl is selling another". One of the girls kept a diary and after the mother read it, accused me of kidnapping the daughter and forcing her into prostitution. After the girl testified how her mother was always on her case for money and indirectly was pressuring her to prostitute herself, I was released

Making a Bank Roll

I would not consider myself, merely a prostitute because I also made big money by robbing the "bank" (a John). This way, I would make several hundred dollars a night that supported an expensive habit. I handled myself real well, never needing a pimp and keeping it all for myself. If you figure that I have been out there for fourteen years, probably more then a million dollars has passed and disappeared through my hands.

A good example of how I operated was with my "biggest bank roll"; a famous actor, named "R". I met him in a restaurant. I was sitting there next to a jostler (pickpocket) who also spotted this mark. I decided to get to him first. I was decently dressed and looked sexy and attractive. He was slightly intoxicated but not so bad to be unaware that he was carrying a load of fifties; enough to choke a horse. While he was preparing to pay, I moved closer to him. He made a gesture to cover some Black dude's bill, telling him "don't worry, we are all brothers". The dude saw it as a put down, but I intervened, telling him, "you should be happy that someone is generous". "R" then turned and thanked me and asked if I recognized who he was. After receiving his acknowledgement, he then bragged of being a great "lover". I listened with phony admiration. We then started rapping, and somewhat suspiciously, he questioned me, "I hope you are not here with none of those pimps or guys who might rob me…..blah, blah, blah?" "Hey come on" I responded, "did you see me sitting with anybody; I'm alone?" We rapped some more and I told him that "I've been listening to that black bro shit all my life and it doesn't mean nothing". It's just like putting your hands in a bowl and there is no bottom." He seemed to like my rap and invited me back to his pad on Park Avenue.

The doorman greeted him and I felt like "Pretty Baby". Here it was a freezing November night, I was without a coat and I am prepared to enter a famous actor's flat. The "scumbag" lived in a studio. Once inside, he got kind of rough, telling me, "I see what you are into but now that you know who I am, you must realize that I don't have to pay for pussy". Flattering him, I agreed. While we were talking, I noted that after he removed his coat, he slipped out his "wad" and went to the bathroom. I watched him stuff the money under the sink like it was dirty clothes. We rapped the night without even making love. He got more and more stone from the booze. In the morning, I gave him a story that I gotta leave to get my kids and excused myself to go to the bathroom. I slipped my hand under the cabinet door and grabbed the bills. He was too wasted to notice.

I took all of it, except for the fifty I left him. The previous day, I only had one hundred dollars to my name and now it is eight in the morning and I am leaving with six thousand dollars in my pocket. Of course, it quickly disappeared. One thousand dollars went to my mother. I then went on a wild spending spree. My philosophy is "easy come, easy go"; when you have money like that, you use it as an opportunity to buy everything.

Murder

Even when money pours in, life on the street has a hard side. I ended up spending five years in prison because I helped murder a girl.

My girlfriend Midnight and I had a three room pad but there were about ten working girls moving in and out of there. A neighborhood Black girl, Lois, started staying over. One night, Midnight woke up to check her dope stash and found along with the loss of sixty dollars, half of it was gone. We search around and I made it clear to Midnight, "I don't want you to think I am going to ignore this robbery; it is both our problems". Midnight understood that it wasn't me. We had been through hell together and intended to burn whoever did this". Now Midnight was not a person to mess with; she was deadly. She could be smiling and at the same time walk up with a "45" and blow your head off.

At first we kept quiet when Lois returned. She claimed she "copped" some dope. Well I knew damn well it was "bullshit". But we let her relax while we waited like spiders to build our web. We watched her wash up, change clothes and followed her downstairs. There she started rapping and bragging. Now Midnight got real pissed and called for her man, Billy, who carried her gun. I heard him say "what do you need it for" but she steered him down, demanding it. Then she asked to see my knife. Turning around, I noticed a patrol car and told her to cool it. After it passed, Midnight approached Lois and told her, "bitch, you got my stuff". Lois then started getting nasty and that set me off, reminding me of my father when he was mean. She was disrespectful and challenged us; "you two think you're bad". I exploded and stabbed her twice in the chest. At first she didn't fall but just stood there with blood gushing and then Midnight pulled out the 45. No questions, nothing; just shot her dead.

Midnight grabbed me by the arm and we jumped into a cab that was driving down 102nd St. Boy, did we pick a winner; it was an anti-crime cab. The cop looked through the rear view mirror, smirking at Midnight with her gun right on her lap. We both did the same time; five years.

We are still friends and in fact, she recently had a baby girl. When we are teamed up, nothing stops or scares us. Like just several months ago, we ripped off a connection for enough coke to stuff a horse. We're aware that one day a "burnt" pusher will blow us away; sooner or later it will happen.

I Want This Baby

It was a surprise to find out I was pregnant. I was watching this guy buy a six pack and noticed he had a wad of bills. I just walked up and took it. There was no hassle; I just threatened him; "I don't want no problems out of you; just turn it over". Bluffing, I told him my backup was nearby waiting in the street. He apparently knew me from the neighborhood and responded, "I know who you are; just don't hurt me". I beat the dude for nine hundred dollars. Running out before he would realize there was no backup, I slipped. Both arms and legs were fractured and I sprained my back. In the hospital I also complained about stomach pain and the first doctor diagnosed it as an ulcer. What a crock of shit some of these doctors are. They finally discovered I was five month's pregnant.

I really want this baby. I am determined to go straight and cut out the drugs. I have had two miscarriages and I can no longer afford to take chances. Right now I am living in a frigid, empty apartment in an abandoned building but I know I can make it. There are a lot of junkies around and when I was hospitalized they stripped the apartment but now that I am back, they don't mess with me. I have been a terror since childhood. I have little hands but they pack a hell of punch. I don't hit like some little girl. I believe because I am bisexual this gives me the strength of a man. I can swing a bat as a weapon like any man. If that doesn't work, well I have stabbed, shot and "razored" my way through life. If any junky bothered me, I'd just do him in and it would be considered self defense; with this pregnancy, those junkies will find themselves facing a wild tiger. I am going to survive no matter what.

I want you to know that I am not alone in this world. There is Jim, who is the most important person in my life. Since he got out of jail, I have been by his side. An ex-junkie, he was doing a life term for killing cop here on First Avenue. Because he is in the last stage of kidney failure, they let him out. Right now, it is only the dialysis machines that keep him alive. He was totally alone when he got out and I knew he needed somebody. Sure he has kids but they are only around when they need some money and at this point he has nothing to give. I am his "darling". Sex is no longer possible but he does try to satisfy me in other ways. Over time, we've become really tight and comfortable with each other. He knew before I got big with the pregnancy I was out on the street. But it was okay with him since it involved blow jobs and this occurred only as a means to rip off the John. We have known each other for a long time and we trust and count on each other. For example, I went into premature labor and despite his illness, he helped carry me down the stairs and got me to the hospital. However I am not going to learn on him. I don't know who the father is but it doesn't matter, my life is going to be determined by my strength alone

Now that I'm pregnant, all I want is a chance. I need welfare to pay for a decent place because I don't want to return to the streets and the empty building. I am not as fit and can no longer be out there freezing my ass. I don't want to live in a place where I have to walk out to the fire hydrant and fill up a pot in order to wash myself. I am not begging and never before asked for help from welfare or any agency. But for once I need to be really helped. I want a new life because there is someone to live for. I pray that I am given that chance.

0-595-32764-8